The History of Weapons

Crafted by Skriuwer

Table of Contents

6. The Introduction of Gunpowder

6.1 The Invention of Gunpowder: A Global Shift

6.2 Early Firearms: From Hand Cannons to Matchlocks

6.3 Gunpowder Artillery: The Birth of Modern Siege Warfare

6.4 The Decline of Traditional Weaponry

6.5 The Spread of Gunpowder Technology Across Cultures

7. Renaissance and Early Modern Weaponry

7.1 The Evolution of Firearms: Flintlocks and Muskets

7.2 The Role of Artillery in Early Modern Warfare

7.3 The Development of Naval Warfare: Ships and Cannons

7.4 The Duel: Honor and Weapons in the Early Modern Era

7.5 The Impact of Weaponry on Exploration and Colonization

8. Industrial Revolution and the Rise of Modern Warfare

8.1 The Impact of the Industrial Revolution on Weapons Manufacturing

8.2 The Introduction of Rifled Firearms: Accuracy and Range

8.3 The Machine Gun: A New Era of Firepower

8.4 The Role of Railways and Logistics in Modern Warfare

8.5 The Evolution of Naval and Artillery Technology

9. World War I: The Birth of Total War

9.1 The Trench Warfare Experience: Rifles, Bayonets, and Grenades

9.2 The Introduction of Chemical Warfare: Weapons of Mass Destruction

9.3 The Tank: Breaking the Stalemate

9.4 Aerial Combat: The Dawn of Military Aviation

9.5 Naval Warfare in WWI: Submarines and Battleships

10. Interwar Period: Innovations and Preparations

10.1 The Rise of Mechanized Warfare: Tanks and Armored Vehicles

10.2 The Evolution of Aircraft: Fighters, Bombers, and Reconnaissance

10.3 The Development of Naval Power: Aircraft Carriers and Battleships

10.4 The Role of Small Arms in Modernizing Armies

10.5 The Role of Intelligence and Espionage

11. World War II: The Global Conflict

11.1 Infantry Weapons of WWII: Rifles, Machine Guns, and Grenades
11.2 Armored Warfare: The Tank Battles of WWII
11.3 Air Superiority: The Role of Aircraft in WWII
11.4 Naval Warfare in WWII: Submarines, Aircraft Carriers, and Battleships
11.5 The Manhattan Project: The Development of Nuclear Weapons

12. The Cold War and the Nuclear Arms Race

12.1 The Dawn of the Nuclear Age: Hiroshima and Nagasaki
12.2 The Arms Race: Building the Nuclear Arsenal
12.3 The Role of Ballistic Missiles and Delivery Systems
12.4 Proxy Wars: Conventional Weapons in the Cold War
12.5 The Threat of Mutually Assured Destruction

13. Post-Cold War and Modern Warfare

13.1 The Evolution of Precision-Guided Munitions
13.2 The Role of Drones in Modern Combat
13.3 Cyber Warfare: A New Frontier
13.4 The Continued Role of Conventional Weapons
13.5 The Ethics and Legalities of Modern Weapons

14. Weapons of the 21st Century

14.1 The Development of Autonomous Weapons: Robots on the Battlefield
14.2 Directed-Energy Weapons: Lasers and Beyond
14.3 Hypersonic Weapons: The New Arms Race
14.4 Space as the Next Battlefield: Weaponizing Space
14.5 The Future of Military Technology: What's Next?

15. The Impact of Weapons on Society

15.1 Weapons and Social Hierarchy: Power and Control
15.2 Weapons and Law: The Regulation of Arms
15.3 The Role of Weapons in Revolutions and Resistance
15.4 The Ethics of Weapon Development and Use
15.5 Weapons in Popular Culture: Myths and Realities

16. The Global Arms Trade

16.1 The Economics of Weaponry: Supply and Demand
16.2 The Role of Governments in the Arms Trade
16.3 The Impact of the Arms Trade on Global Conflicts
16.4 The Illegal Arms Trade: Black Markets and Smuggling
16.5 Efforts to Control the Global Arms Trade

17. Weapons and Human Rights

17.1 The Human Cost of Weapons: War and Civilians
17.2 The Use of Weapons in Genocide and Ethnic Cleansing
17.3 The Debate Over Landmines and Cluster Munitions
17.4 Arms Control and Disarmament Efforts
17.5 The Future of Weapons and Human Rights: Challenges Ahead

18. The Role of Weapons in Peacekeeping and Security

18.1 Weapons in Peacekeeping Operations: Tools for Stability or Conflict?
18.2 Disarmament and Demobilization: Post-Conflict Weapon Collection
18.3 The Role of Non-Lethal Weapons in Modern Security
18.4 The Challenge of Small Arms Proliferation
18.5 The Future of Global Security: Weapons and Diplomacy

19. Weapons in the Age of Terrorism

19.1 The Use of Weapons by Terrorist Organizations
19.2 The Threat of Nuclear, Biological, and Chemical Weapons
19.3 The Role of Technology in Counter-Terrorism
19.4 Cyberterrorism: The Digital Weapon
19.5 The Global Response to Terrorism: Weapons and Tactics

20. Conclusion: The Future of Weapons and Warfare

20.1 The Continuous Evolution of Weaponry
20.2 Ethical Considerations in Future Weapon Development
20.3 The Role of International Law in Weapon Regulation
20.4 Preparing for the Unknown: Emerging Threats
20.5 Final Thoughts: The Balance Between Security and Humanity

<h1 align="center">Chapter 1</h1>

<h1 align="center">The Origins of Weaponry</h1>

The First Tools

The evolution of weaponry traces back to the very dawn of humanity when early humans began to adapt simple tools for hunting and defense. The transition from rudimentary tools to sophisticated weapons marked a pivotal moment in human history, influencing survival, social organization, and the development of culture.

The Origins of Stone Tools

Approximately 2.6 million years ago, early hominins, such as Homo habilis, began to craft the first stone tools, known as Oldowan tools. These primitive implements were primarily used for scavenging and butchering animals, facilitating access to meat and fat that were essential for survival. The simplest of these tools consisted of sharp-edged stones that could be struck against one another to create cutting implements.

As humans evolved, so did their tool-making techniques. The Acheulean tool industry, which emerged around 1.76 million years ago, introduced bifacial hand axes, characterized by their symmetrical shapes and sharp edges. These axes were not only vital for butchery but also served defensive purposes against predators and rival groups. The ability to create more advanced tools demonstrated an increasing cognitive capacity, allowing early humans to manipulate their environment effectively.

Adaptation for Hunting

The adaptation of tools for hunting was a significant advancement that allowed early humans to become proficient hunters. The development of spears, made by attaching sharpened stone points to wooden shafts, marked a transformative leap in hunting technology. These weapons provided greater reach and lethality, enabling early humans to target larger game, which was crucial for sustaining growing communities. By employing thrusting and throwing techniques, early humans could hunt from a safer distance, reducing the risk of injury from dangerous animals.

The introduction of composite tools, such as the atlatl (a spear-throwing device), further enhanced hunting efficiency. This innovation allowed for increased force and distance when launching projectiles, making it possible to hunt with even greater success. The ability to adapt tools for specific hunting strategies showcased the ingenuity and resourcefulness of early humans, laying the groundwork for future developments in weaponry.

Defensive Applications

The creation of tools was not solely focused on hunting; defense against potential threats was equally important. Early humans faced dangers from both wild animals and rival tribes. Thus, tools were adapted for defensive purposes, with pointed sticks and sharpened stones serving as makeshift weapons in confrontations. The need for protection led to the development of strategies for group defense, where tools and weapons were used collectively to safeguard communities.

Moreover, the gradual transition from individual survival to communal living necessitated a more organized approach to both hunting and defense. Social dynamics began to shift as groups formed, leading to the emergence of social hierarchies and roles within these early communities. As humans realized the importance of cooperation, the tools they created became symbols of shared resources and collective strength, ultimately shaping the interactions between different groups.

Conclusion

The journey from simple stone tools to weapons illustrates the remarkable adaptability of early humans. These initial adaptations for hunting and defense not only ensured survival but also laid the foundation for the complex societies that would follow. As tool-making evolved, it spurred technological advancements and influenced social structures, highlighting the profound impact that weaponry has had on human history. The legacy of these first tools continues to resonate in contemporary discussions about technology, warfare, and the human condition, reminding us that the origins of weaponry are deeply embedded in the narrative of our species.

The Development of Spears and Clubs

The development of spears and clubs marked a significant milestone in the evolution of weaponry during prehistoric times. As early humans transitioned from foraging to more structured forms of hunting and defense, the need for effective tools became paramount. Spears and clubs emerged as fundamental weapons that not only enhanced hunting efficiency but also played pivotal roles in social and territorial conflicts.

Origins and Early Design

The earliest hand-held weapons, primarily clubs, were rudimentary tools crafted from readily available materials such as wood and stone. These primitive weapons were simply fashioned by selecting sturdy branches or logs, sometimes with sharpened ends for increased lethality. The club provided an immediate advantage in close combat situations, allowing early humans to defend themselves against predators or rival groups.

As societies evolved, so too did the complexity of these weapons. The spear, characterized by a pointed end, emerged as an essential hunting tool. Initially, spears were made from sharpened sticks, but advancements in tool-making led to the incorporation of stone points. These spearheads were affixed to wooden shafts, increasing their effectiveness in hunting large game. Archaeological findings indicate that the development of the spear significantly improved the range and accuracy of early hunters, allowing them to strike prey from a distance, thus reducing the risk of injury from dangerous animals.

Technological Innovations
The introduction of hafting—the process of attaching a stone or bone point to a wooden shaft—marked a revolutionary step in weapon design. This technique not only improved the durability of spears but also enhanced their lethality, as the sharp points could penetrate the hides of large animals. Evidence from various prehistoric sites illustrates the diversity of spear designs, with some featuring barbed points intended to prevent prey from escaping once struck.

Furthermore, the evolution of materials played a crucial role in the development of these weapons. As humans learned to manipulate fire, they began to harden wood by charring it, creating stronger shafts for their spears. The discovery of metallurgy later introduced the use of bronze and iron spearheads, which further revolutionized weaponry, increasing the lethality and effectiveness of spears in both hunting and warfare.

Social Implications
The advent of spears and clubs had profound social implications. These weapons were not merely tools for survival; they became symbols of power and status within prehistoric communities. Possession of effective weaponry often correlated with an individual's or group's ability to provide for their community, defend their territory, and exert influence over others. The use of spears, in particular, facilitated organized hunting strategies and collective defense mechanisms, fostering cooperation among early human groups.

Moreover, the development of these weapons also contributed to social stratification. As certain individuals became skilled hunters or warriors, they gained prestige and authority, leading to the emergence of early leadership roles. The ability to wield a spear effectively became a marker of strength and capability, shaping social dynamics within communities.

Conclusion
The development of spears and clubs represents a fundamental phase in the history of weaponry, illustrating the ingenuity and adaptability of early humans. These simple yet effective tools laid the groundwork for more complex weapon systems that would emerge in subsequent eras. By enhancing hunting capabilities and altering social structures, spears and clubs not only played a critical role in survival but also became integral to the cultural and social evolution of prehistoric societies. As such, they remain a testament to humanity's enduring relationship with technology, conflict, and community.

The Bow and Arrow

The invention of the bow and arrow marked a pivotal turning point in the evolution of weaponry and warfare, fundamentally altering both hunting practices and combat strategies. Emerging around 20,000 years ago, the bow and arrow allowed early humans to engage targets at a distance, significantly enhancing their ability to hunt and defend against predators or rival groups. The implications of this innovation extended far beyond mere survival; it transformed the dynamics of social organization and military tactics.

The Mechanics and Advantages of the Bow and Arrow

The bow, a flexible weapon made from a curved piece of wood with a string attached, works by storing energy when drawn and releasing it to propel an arrow. Arrows, typically made from lightweight materials such as wood, feathers, and stone or metal tips, could be crafted for specific purposes, including hunting large game or engaging in combat. The bow's ability to shoot projectiles at high velocity and over considerable distances gave its users a significant tactical advantage. Unlike melee weapons, which required close proximity to the target, archery allowed warriors to strike from a distance, minimizing personal risk and increasing the element of surprise.

Transformation of Hunting Practices

In the context of hunting, the bow and arrow revolutionized the way early humans gathered food. Prior to its invention, hunters relied primarily on spears and clubs, which necessitated close encounters with dangerous prey. The bow allowed for a more strategic approach to hunting, enabling hunters to engage large game such as deer, elk, and even mammoths without exposing themselves to danger. This advancement not only improved efficiency in hunting but also allowed for greater food security and the ability to target more formidable game, which could support larger communities.

Impact on Warfare

The introduction of the bow and arrow into warfare had dramatic consequences for human conflict. The ability to engage enemies from a distance changed the nature of battle, leading to the development of new tactics and formations. Armies began to incorporate archers into their ranks, recognizing the value of ranged combat. The bow became a staple in the arsenals of various civilizations, from the ancient Egyptians to the Mongols, each refining its design and tactics to maximize its effectiveness in battle.

Archers could harass enemy forces, disrupt formations, and provide cover for advancing troops. The psychological impact of a well-coordinated volley of arrows could demoralize opponents, often leading to routs before a direct confrontation even occurred. The use of archers also contributed to the evolution of protective gear, such as shields and armor, as armies adapted to counter this new threat.

Tactical Innovations

As warfare evolved, so did the technology surrounding the bow. Innovations such as the composite bow, which combined materials like wood, horn, and sinew, allowed for greater power and compactness. This made the bow more efficient and portable, further enhancing its role on the battlefield. The introduction of crossbows in the later periods of history represented another significant development, enabling even less trained individuals to effectively utilize ranged weaponry against armored foes.

The bow and arrow not only transformed hunting and combat but also significantly influenced social structures. Societies that mastered archery often gained military superiority, leading to territorial expansion and the establishment of empires. The training of archers became a vital part of military culture, and archery contests emerged as popular social events, reinforcing its importance in both martial and community contexts.

Conclusion

In summary, the bow and arrow stands out as a groundbreaking advancement in the history of weaponry. Its capacity to change the nature of both hunting and warfare allowed early civilizations to thrive, shaping military strategies and societal hierarchies for centuries to come. The legacy of the bow and arrow is evident in the continued evolution of ranged weaponry, demonstrating its lasting impact on human conflict and cooperation.

Early Fortifications and Siege Weapons

Throughout human history, the quest for security and the protection of resources has driven the development of defensive structures, commonly known as fortifications. These structures emerged as early humans settled into more permanent communities, transitioning from nomadic lifestyles and seeking to safeguard their homes and livelihoods from rival groups and natural threats. The evolution of fortifications is intimately linked to the development of siege weapons—devices designed to breach these defenses—marking a pivotal point in the history of warfare.

The Rise of Fortifications

The earliest forms of fortifications can be traced back to ancient settlements where natural barriers such as rivers, cliffs, and dense forests provided initial protection. As communities grew and conflicts arose, humans began to enhance their defenses. Early fortifications included simple earthworks, wooden palisades, and stone walls, constructed to deter attacks from marauding bands. The walls were often elevated, creating a vantage point for defenders and a formidable obstacle for would-be attackers.

As societies advanced, particularly during the Bronze and Iron Ages, fortifications became more sophisticated. The development of masonry techniques allowed for the construction of high stone walls, reinforced with towers and gates. These structures were not just practical; they also served as symbols of power and stability, reflecting the wealth and strength of the community. Cities like Uruk in Mesopotamia and Thebes in ancient Egypt exemplified the use of massive walls as both a protective measure and a demonstration of urban sophistication.

The Birth of Siege Weapons
As fortifications grew more complex, so too did the weapons designed to overcome them. Siege warfare became a specialized field, leading to the invention of various siege engines that could breach fortified walls. The earliest siege weapons included battering rams, which were heavy beams swung or pushed against gates or walls to create openings. These devices required a coordinated effort from attackers and often necessitated the construction of protective structures to shield operators from defenders' projectiles.

The introduction of catapults and ballistae marked a significant advancement in siege technology. Catapults, such as the onager and the trebuchet, were capable of launching projectiles over walls, allowing besiegers to strike at defenders from a distance. The trebuchet, in particular, revolutionized siege warfare with its counterweight mechanism, providing greater range and power compared to earlier torsion-based devices. As these weapons became more prevalent, the dynamics of warfare shifted, as attackers could now engage fortifications from a safer distance.

The Tactical Implications of Fortifications and Siege Warfare
The interplay between fortifications and siege weapons significantly impacted military strategy. Defenders could rely on their walls to provide safety and to control the battlefield, while attackers had to devise strategies to effectively breach these defenses. The siege became a protracted affair, often lasting weeks or months, as both sides engaged in a battle of attrition, employing deception, psychological warfare, and resource management.

Moreover, the development of fortifications led to the emergence of siegecraft as a tactical discipline. Engineers and military leaders studied the strengths and weaknesses of different fortifications, leading to innovations in siege tactics and the design of effective siege engines. The ability to breach a fortified city often determined the outcome of conflicts, influencing the rise and fall of kingdoms.

Conclusion
The origins of defensive structures and the tools to breach them illustrate a fundamental aspect of human conflict: the interplay between offense and defense. As societies evolved and technologies advanced, so too did the strategies and tools of warfare. The development of early fortifications and siege weapons not only shaped the landscape of ancient combat but also laid the groundwork for the complex military strategies that would dominate later eras. This

ongoing cycle of innovation and adaptation continues to resonate in contemporary military practices, reminding us of the enduring nature of conflict and the relentless pursuit of security.

The Role of Weaponry in Early Human Societies

The advent of weaponry marked a pivotal turning point in the course of human history, profoundly influencing social structures and power dynamics within early human societies. As early humans evolved from simple hunter-gatherers to more complex social groups, the development and use of weapons played a crucial role in shaping their interactions, hierarchies, and overall societal organization.

Weaponry as a Status Symbol

In prehistoric societies, the possession of weapons was not merely a matter of survival; it often signified status and power. For instance, individuals who could create or obtain superior weapons, such as finely crafted spears or bows, held a place of esteem within their communities. This dynamic fostered a form of social stratification, where those skilled in weapon-making or proficient in their use gained prominence, leading to the emergence of specialized roles. As these weapons became symbols of strength and capability, leaders or chiefs often distinguished themselves through their prowess in hunting or warfare, thereby consolidating power and influence within their groups.

Weapons and Territoriality

The use of weapons also fundamentally altered the notions of territory and resource control. As communities transitioned from nomadic lifestyles to settled agriculture, the competition for land and resources became increasingly pronounced. Weapons such as clubs and spears were employed not only for hunting but also for defending territories against rival groups. This territoriality necessitated the establishment of social norms and rules, leading to the development of early forms of governance and organized conflict. Thus, weaponry was instrumental in delineating boundaries and asserting dominance, prompting societies to develop strategies for both offense and defense.

Power Dynamics Among Groups

Weaponry also influenced interactions between different groups, shaping alliances and rivalries. The ability to wield weapons effectively could determine whether a group emerged as dominant or subordinate. For example, tribes that mastered the use of bows and arrows could hunt more efficiently and defend themselves more effectively than those who relied solely on primitive tools. This superiority in weaponry could lead to the expansion of territory, the acquisition of resources, and the subjugation of weaker groups. Consequently, the dynamics of power shifted based on the technological advancements in weaponry, leading to the rise and fall of various tribes and societies throughout history.

Cultural Significance and Ritualization

Beyond practical implications, weapons also held cultural significance within early human societies. Many communities developed rituals and practices surrounding the creation and use of weapons, which often became intertwined with their identities and belief systems. Weapons were imbued with symbolic meanings, representing not only power but also cultural values such as bravery, honor, and protection. This cultural dimension reinforced social cohesion within groups, as shared beliefs about weaponry could unify members and define their collective identity in contrast to others.

Conflict and Cooperation

The dual nature of weaponry as a tool for both conflict and cooperation is another critical aspect of its role in early human societies. While weapons enabled violence and warfare, they also facilitated negotiation, trade, and alliances. Communities that possessed advanced weaponry could engage in complex exchanges with neighboring groups, establishing trade routes and diplomatic relationships. In this sense, weaponry was not only a catalyst for conflict but also a means of fostering cooperation, as groups recognized the benefits of mutual protection and resource sharing in a world marked by competition and uncertainty.

In conclusion, the role of weaponry in early human societies was multifaceted, influencing social structures, power dynamics, and cultural identities. As weapons evolved, so too did the complexities of human interactions, laying the groundwork for the intricate social systems that would characterize later civilizations. The interplay between weapons, status, territory, and cultural significance underscores the profound impact that tools of violence have had on human development and societal organization throughout history.

Chapter 2

Bronze Age Weaponry

The Introduction of Bronze

The discovery of bronze marked a pivotal moment in the history of weaponry, transforming not only the tools of war but also the very fabric of societies that wielded them. Bronze, an alloy primarily made of copper and tin, first emerged around 3300 BCE in the Near East, initiating what is now known as the Bronze Age. This era was characterized by significant advancements in metallurgy, which facilitated the production of stronger, more durable weapons compared to their stone and copper predecessors.

The Metallurgical Revolution

Prior to the advent of bronze, early civilizations relied heavily on stone tools and weapons, such as flint blades and wooden clubs. While effective for their time, these materials had limitations in terms of durability and effectiveness. The introduction of bronze allowed for the creation of weapons that were not only sharper but also capable of withstanding greater impact without breaking or warping. The superior properties of bronze, including its ability to be cast into intricate shapes, led to the development of more complex weapon designs, such as swords, spears, and axes.

Bronze weapons offered several advantages over their stone and copper counterparts. The alloy's hardness enabled weapons to maintain sharp edges for longer periods, enhancing their lethality in combat. For instance, bronze swords could slice through armor and flesh with far greater efficiency than stone blades, significantly changing the dynamics of warfare.

Military Innovations

As bronze weaponry became widespread, it also catalyzed changes in military tactics and organization. Armies began to adopt standardized weapons, which contributed to more cohesive and effective fighting forces. The introduction of bronze-cast weapons allowed for the creation of mass-produced armaments, leading to larger and better-equipped armies. The ability to produce weapons en masse was a game-changer for many ancient civilizations, enabling states to exert power over larger territories and engage in prolonged conflicts.

This period saw the rise of significant military formations, such as the phalanx in ancient Greece and the legions of Rome, both of which relied on the effectiveness of bronze weapons to maintain their dominance on the battlefield. Bronze spearheads and swords became symbols of power, often reserved for the elite warrior classes, reinforcing social hierarchies that revolved around martial prowess.

Economic and Social Impacts
The shift to bronze weaponry also had profound economic implications. The demand for copper and tin spurred trade networks, as these materials were not always readily available in local regions. The need to source these metals led to the emergence of long-distance trade routes, allowing for cultural exchanges and the spread of technological innovations. As civilizations interacted through trade, they shared not only materials but also techniques for metallurgy and weapon-making, further enhancing the quality and effectiveness of bronze weaponry.

Additionally, the social structures of societies evolved in response to the changes brought about by bronze. The concentration of weapon production and trade often led to the establishment of specialized craftspeople and a merchant class, shifting the dynamics of power within communities. As societies became more stratified, the role of the warrior elite grew, further entrenching the relationship between military capability and social status.

Conclusion
In conclusion, the introduction of bronze as a material for weapon-making heralded a new era in military history. The enhanced properties of bronze weapons enabled advancements in warfare tactics, military organization, and economic systems, fundamentally altering the course of human civilization. The legacy of this metallurgical revolution resonates through the ages, shaping not only the strategies of war but also the power dynamics within societies. As such, the transition from stone to bronze marks a significant milestone in the evolution of weaponry, one that paved the way for future innovations in military technology.

Swords and Daggers
The advent of bronze marked a pivotal moment in the history of weaponry, particularly in the development of bladed weapons such as swords and daggers. The transition from stone to bronze not only represented a technological revolution but also transformed the dynamics of warfare, social status, and power hierarchies within ancient civilizations.

Bronze, an alloy typically composed of copper and tin, offered distinct advantages over its predecessors. It was more durable and could be cast and shaped into sharper, more effective blades. This allowed for the production of weapons that were not only lethal but also capable of being mass-produced, which was essential for the burgeoning armies of the time. The creation of bronze bladed weapons facilitated advancements in combat techniques, enabling soldiers to wield their weapons with greater efficiency and skill.

The sword emerged as a significant symbol of power and status in ancient societies. Unlike simpler weapons such as spears or clubs, swords required specialized craftsmanship and skill to produce. This exclusivity meant that swords were often associated with the elite, including warriors, nobility, and leaders. In many cultures, owning a sword was a mark of honor and prestige, signifying one's role as a protector or warrior within the community. The craftsmanship involved in creating a sword often involved intricate designs and decorations, further enhancing its status as a symbol of power.

Daggers, on the other hand, served both practical and symbolic purposes. These shorter blades were ideal for close-quarters combat and were often used in stealth operations or for personal defense. In many cultures, daggers were imbued with symbolic significance, often carried by individuals as a mark of status or as part of ceremonial dress. They were sometimes used in rituals or as offerings to deities, reflecting their importance beyond mere functionality.

The development of bronze swords and daggers also influenced military strategies and tactics. Armies began to organize around the use of these weapons, leading to the formation of specialized combat units, such as those armed with swords for close combat. The effectiveness of bronze blades in battle contributed to the establishment of professional standing armies, which shifted the nature of warfare from individual tribal skirmishes to organized military campaigns.

As bronze weaponry spread across various civilizations, it facilitated cultural exchange and the sharing of military techniques. Societies that adopted bronze swords and daggers often incorporated them into their own unique combat styles and rituals. For instance, the Greek hoplites, heavily armed infantrymen, relied on the combination of bronze swords and shields to create formidable phalanx formations. Similarly, the Celts developed their own distinctive styles of sword-making, characterized by intricate designs and robust blades, which became symbols of their warrior culture.

Moreover, the significance of bronze bladed weapons transcended the battlefield. In many ancient societies, the sword became a cultural icon, representing justice, chivalry, and honor. Literature and mythology often depicted swords as embodiments of power and destiny, such as Excalibur in Arthurian legend or the swords of various gods and heroes in ancient epics.

In conclusion, the development of bronze swords and daggers was not merely a technological advancement; it was a transformative force that shaped the social and military landscapes of ancient civilizations. These weapons became symbols of power, status, and cultural identity, influencing everything from personal honor to the strategies of warfare. Their legacy continues to resonate in modern interpretations of combat and the symbolism of weaponry, underscoring the enduring impact of these bronze bladed weapons on human history.

The Chariot

The chariot represents one of the most transformative innovations in ancient warfare, forever altering the dynamics of military strategy and battlefield mobility. Emerging around 2000 BCE in the Near East, chariots quickly revolutionized the way armies maneuvered and engaged in combat. This two-wheeled vehicle, typically drawn by horses, enabled a new form of warfare characterized by speed, mobility, and tactical flexibility.

Origins and Design

The earliest chariots were developed from simpler two-wheeled carts and were initially used for transportation and trade. However, as societies became more complex and warfare more prevalent, the design evolved. The introduction of the horse as a draft animal was crucial; it provided the necessary power to propel the chariot at greater speeds than previously possible. Chariots were usually constructed from wood, reinforced with leather, and often equipped with spoked wheels, which significantly reduced the weight and increased maneuverability.

By the time of the Middle Bronze Age, chariots had become a standard component of military forces in civilizations such as the Hittites, Egyptians, and Mesopotamians. In these cultures, chariots were typically manned by a driver and an archer or spearman, allowing for a combination of mobility and firepower that transformed battlefield tactics.

Tactical Advantages

The introduction of the chariot provided distinct advantages in combat. With their speed and agility, chariots could outmaneuver heavier infantry formations, striking swiftly and retreating before a counterattack could be mounted. This capability allowed chariot forces to execute hit-and-run tactics, disrupting enemy formations and targeting vulnerable units. Furthermore, the elevated position of the charioteer and the archer provided a significant advantage in visibility, allowing for more precise targeting and coordination during engagements.

Chariots also played a critical role in the organization of armies. Their presence often dictated the formation of opposing forces; infantry units were increasingly required to adapt to the threat posed by mobile chariotry. Consequently, armies began to develop specialized units to counter chariot threats, leading to a dynamic evolution of military tactics.

Cultural and Political Implications
The significance of chariots extended beyond the battlefield. They became symbols of power and prestige, often associated with royalty and elite warriors. In many ancient cultures, owning a chariot was a sign of status; thus, they were not only tools of war but also representations of wealth and influence. Chariotry often dictated social hierarchies, as those who could afford horses and chariots held higher positions within their societies.

The strategic use of chariots also had profound implications for the political landscape. Kingdoms and empires that effectively utilized chariot warfare gained substantial advantages over their rivals, leading to the expansion of territories and the establishment of dominance in the region. Notable examples include the Egyptian Pharaohs, who harnessed chariotry to secure victories against rival states, solidifying their rule and expanding their empire.

The Decline of the Chariot
Despite its revolutionary impact, the chariot's prominence began to wane by the end of the Iron Age, as advancements in infantry tactics and technology, including the development of more effective armor and the introduction of the cavalry, began to overshadow its utility. By the time of the Classical period, the chariot had largely been replaced by mounted warriors as the primary mobile force in armies.

Conclusion
In summary, the chariot was a groundbreaking innovation that reshaped ancient warfare. Its introduction not only enhanced battlefield mobility but also influenced social structures and political dynamics across various civilizations. The legacy of chariotry is evident in the way it set the stage for future military developments, demonstrating the profound impact of technological advancements on the conduct of war throughout history.

The Emergence of Body Armor and Shields
The evolution of weaponry is intrinsically linked to the development of defensive gear, particularly body armor and shields. As early humans transitioned from rudimentary tools to more sophisticated weaponry for hunting and warfare, the need for protection grew correspondingly. This dynamic interplay between offensive and defensive technologies played a pivotal role in shaping ancient combat strategies and societal structures.

Historical Context

The earliest forms of body armor can be traced back to prehistoric societies, where humans utilized natural materials such as animal hides, leather, and woven fabrics. These primitive forms of protection were designed to mitigate injuries from stone weapons and sharpened implements used in hunting and combat. As communities grew and warfare became more organized, the demand for effective defensive gear intensified. The introduction of metalworking marks a significant milestone in the evolution of body armor. During the Bronze Age, warriors began to craft armor from bronze, a material that offered greater durability and protection compared to its predecessors. This advancement not only enhanced individual safety but also influenced military tactics, as armies could now field heavily armored soldiers capable of withstanding greater assaults.

The Role of Shields

Shields have played a crucial role in the development of defensive strategies. Initially made from wood and leather, the shield evolved into a vital component of a warrior's arsenal. As weaponry advanced, particularly with the introduction of metal swords and spears, shields were reinforced with metal, providing enhanced protection. The design and size of shields varied across cultures, reflecting regional combat styles and tactical preferences. For instance, the hoplite shield of ancient Greece, known as the "aspis," was large and round, allowing soldiers to form a protective wall in phalanx formations. In contrast, the Roman scutum was a rectangular shield that provided coverage for the entire body and was instrumental in the success of the Roman legions.

Advancements in Body Armor

As societies grew more complex, so too did the armor worn by soldiers. The transition from bronze to iron during the Iron Age heralded a new era of protective gear. Iron armor, although heavier, provided superior defense against the increasingly lethal weapons of the time. The development of chain mail, consisting of interlinked metal rings, represented a significant advance in armor technology. It offered flexibility and mobility while maintaining a high level of protection against slashing and thrusting attacks.

By the medieval period, armor had evolved into full suits, often made of plate metal, that covered the entire body. This evolution allowed knights to engage in direct combat while minimizing the risk of injury. The iconic image of a knight in shining armor symbolizes the peak of medieval defensive technology. However, as firearms emerged in the late medieval period and into the Renaissance, traditional plate armor faced new challenges. The lethality of gunpowder weapons necessitated further innovations in armor design, leading to the creation of reinforced armor that could withstand musket fire.

The Interplay of Offense and Defense
The rise of body armor and shields fundamentally altered the dynamics of warfare. With improved defensive gear, soldiers could engage in prolonged combat, allowing for more strategic and tactical maneuvers. However, this also spurred advancements in offensive weaponry. As armor became more sophisticated, so too did the weapons designed to penetrate it. The development of crossbows, pikes, and later, firearms, reflected this ongoing arms race between offense and defense.

In conclusion, the emergence of body armor and shields marked a significant evolution in military technology that paralleled advancements in offensive weaponry. This relationship was characterized by an ongoing cycle of adaptation and innovation, shaping not only the nature of combat but also the societal structures surrounding warfare. As civilizations progressed, the quest for protection continued to drive developments in defensive gear, underscoring the enduring significance of armor and shields in the historical narrative of weaponry.

The Spread of Bronze Weapons Across Civilizations
The advent of bronze weaponry marked a pivotal moment in human history, transforming not only the nature of warfare but also the sociopolitical landscape of ancient civilizations. The transition from stone and other primitive materials to bronze—an alloy primarily of copper and tin—enabled the production of stronger, more durable weapons. This technological advancement had profound implications for the societies that adopted it, leading to the spread of bronze weapons across different cultures and regions.

Initially, the use of bronze weapons was concentrated in areas rich in the necessary resources, such as the Near East, particularly in regions like Mesopotamia and Anatolia. The first known civilization to exploit bronze extensively was the Sumerians around 3000 BCE. The strength and resilience of bronze allowed for the creation of various tools, including swords, spears, and axes, which were far superior to their stone counterparts. As these early civilizations flourished, the advantages provided by bronze weaponry became evident, leading to a competitive arms race among neighboring societies.

Trade networks played a crucial role in the dissemination of bronze technology. As societies began to recognize the military and economic benefits of bronze weapons, they established extensive trade routes to acquire both the raw materials—copper and tin—and the finished products. The trade routes extended from the Mediterranean to the Indus Valley and beyond, facilitating cultural exchange and the sharing of technological innovations. This interaction not only spread bronze weaponry but also led to the adaptation of these weapons to meet local needs and preferences.

The influence of bronze weaponry can be seen in the military strategies adopted by various cultures. For instance, in ancient Egypt, the introduction of bronze swords and spearheads allowed pharaohs to expand their territories and maintain control over vast regions. The military elite, equipped with these superior weapons, became symbols of power and authority, reinforcing social hierarchies. The Hittites, who rose to prominence in Anatolia, also embraced bronze technology, utilizing it in their chariotry, which became a cornerstone of their military successes against rival states.

As bronze weapons spread, they were often integrated into existing martial traditions. The Minoans and Mycenaeans on the Aegean islands used bronze to create finely crafted weapons and tools that reflected their advanced metallurgy. The Mycenaean warriors, for instance, became known for their bronze armaments, and their military prowess was instrumental in establishing their dominance in the region. This adoption of bronze technology not only transformed warfare but also influenced artistic and cultural expressions, as seen in the intricate designs found on bronze weapons and armor.

The influence of bronze weaponry extended beyond the battlefield; it also shaped trade relations and diplomatic interactions among civilizations. States possessing superior bronze weaponry often exerted influence over their neighbors, leading to alliances, conflicts, and the establishment of empires. The spread of bronze weapons, therefore, was not merely a technological advancement; it was a catalyst for political and cultural transformations.

In summary, the spread of bronze weaponry across civilizations was a significant driver of change in the ancient world. Through trade, military innovation, and cultural exchange, bronze technology reshaped societies, facilitated territorial expansion, and influenced the social dynamics of power and control. The legacy of bronze weaponry is evident in the historical trajectory of many ancient civilizations, marking a transformative era that laid the groundwork for future advancements in weaponry and warfare.

Chapter 3

Iron Age Weaponry

The Iron Revolution

The transition from bronze to iron during the early first millennium BCE marked a seismic shift in the landscape of weaponry and warfare, a transformation often referred to as the Iron Revolution. This period not only ushered in stronger and sharper weapons but also redefined military tactics, social structures, and the very fabric of civilization itself. The advent of iron as the primary material for weapon-making facilitated advancements that would influence warfare for centuries to come.

Metallurgical Advancements

Iron, as a material, is more abundant than copper or tin, the essential components of bronze. Early iron metallurgy emerged around 1200 BCE, initially in regions such as Anatolia and the Caucasus. The ability to smelt iron from its ore at relatively lower temperatures than required for bronze production made it accessible to a wider array of cultures. This accessibility led to the proliferation of iron weapons, which were not only stronger but also more durable and capable of being produced in larger quantities.

The development of techniques such as carburization, where carbon was added to iron to create steel, further enhanced the effectiveness of iron weapons. Steel blades, which were sharper and could hold an edge longer than their bronze counterparts, became a game-changer on the battlefield. This innovation allowed for the production of superior swords, spears, and other weapons, dramatically improving combat effectiveness.

Tactical Implications

The introduction of iron weaponry significantly altered battlefield dynamics. The enhanced strength and sharpness of iron weapons allowed for new combat strategies and formations. Armies equipped with iron weapons could engage more effectively in close-quarters combat, leading to changes in military organization. Heavy infantry armed with iron swords and spears became the backbone of many armies, replacing lighter, less effective units that relied on bronze weaponry.

The use of iron also contributed to the rise of cavalry as a dominant force in warfare. Iron stirrups and weapons allowed mounted warriors to charge with greater force and precision. The impact of a well-trained cavalry unit equipped with iron weapons could turn the tide of battle, leading to a reevaluation of tactics and military formations. Formations such as the phalanx, which had been effective with bronze weaponry, were adapted to incorporate the improved capabilities of iron-armored troops.

Social and Economic Impact

The Iron Revolution had profound social and economic ramifications. The increased availability of iron weapons democratized military power, enabling smaller states and tribes to compete with larger empires that had previously maintained dominance through superior bronze weaponry. This shift contributed to the rise of new political entities and the decline of established ones, as the balance of power fluctuated with the accessibility of iron.

Moreover, the production of iron weapons spurred economic growth through the establishment of ironworking centers, leading to specialized trades and increased trade networks. Societies that adapted to iron production found themselves at an advantage, fostering technological innovation and economic expansion.

Conclusion

The transition from bronze to iron represented more than a mere technological advancement; it was a revolution that reshaped warfare, societal structures, and economies across the globe. Iron's superior qualities allowed for the development of stronger and sharper weapons that not only enhanced combat effectiveness but also altered military tactics and the organization of armies. As iron became the material of choice for weaponry, it laid the groundwork for the military and geopolitical realities of the ancient world, influencing the course of human history for millennia. The Iron Revolution thus stands as a pivotal chapter in the history of weapons, reflecting the intertwined evolution of technology, warfare, and society.

The Evolution of Swords

The sword, a weapon that has captivated the imagination of warriors and historians alike, has undergone significant transformations in its design, material, and functionality from the Iron Age through to the Middle Ages. The evolution from iron to steel swords marks a pivotal shift in weaponry, characterized by advancements in metalworking techniques and a deeper understanding of metallurgy.

The Transition from Iron to Steel

During the Iron Age, which began around 1200 BCE, iron became the dominant material for weaponry, including swords. Early iron swords were forged from wrought iron, a relatively soft and malleable metal. While these iron swords were an improvement over bronze weapons, they suffered from limitations in durability and sharpness. Wrought iron's softness meant that edges could easily become dull or damaged during combat, necessitating frequent maintenance.

The breakthrough came with the eventual introduction of steel, an alloy of iron and carbon that offered superior strength and hardness. The process of creating steel involved controlling the carbon content in iron, which could be achieved through various techniques, including carburization—heating iron in the presence of carbon-rich materials. This process allowed craftsmen to produce blades that were not only sharper but also retained their edge longer than their wrought iron predecessors.

Advancements in Metallurgy

The understanding of metallurgy played a critical role in the development of swords. By the first millennium CE, blacksmiths had begun experimenting with different methods of heating and cooling metals to produce various types of steel. Techniques such as quenching (rapidly cooling hot metal in water or oil) and tempering (slowly reheating to remove brittleness) became standard practices. These methods allowed for the production of blades that were both hard and flexible, optimizing them for the rigors of battle.

One notable form of steel that emerged during this time was pattern-welded steel, produced by forging together layers of different metals, typically iron and steel. This technique not only enhanced the mechanical properties of the blade but also produced striking patterns on the surface, which became a hallmark of fine craftsmanship. The famous Damascus steel, known for its distinctive patterns and exceptional properties, is a historical example of this technique.

The Design Evolution of Swords

As swordmaking techniques progressed, so did the design of the weapons themselves. Early iron swords were often short and broad, designed for slashing or thrusting. However, as the quality of steel improved, swords began to evolve in shape and size. The introduction of longer, more tapered blades allowed for greater thrusting capability, which became particularly advantageous in the context of mounted warfare.

During the medieval period, the emergence of the longsword—characterized by its cruciform hilt and longer blade—reflected changes in combat tactics and armor design. As plate armor became prevalent among knights, swords needed to adapt. The design of swords shifted to include features such as fuller (a groove along the length of the blade that reduces weight while maintaining strength) and cross-guards that enhanced grip and control.

Cultural Significance

The transition from iron to steel swords also had significant cultural implications. Swords became symbols of power, status, and honor, often associated with nobility and knights. The craftsmanship of a sword could signify the skill of its maker, while the ownership of a finely crafted steel sword could denote a warrior's prowess and social standing.

In conclusion, the evolution of swords from iron to steel reflects not only advancements in metalworking but also the broader changes in warfare, social structures, and cultural values throughout history. The development of steel swords marked a new era in weaponry, setting the stage for the iconic swords that would define combat in the medieval world and beyond. As blacksmiths continued to innovate, the sword would remain a central element in the narrative of human conflict and craftsmanship, symbolizing both the art of war and the artistry of its makers.

The Rise of Cavalry

The advent of cavalry marked a pivotal transformation in military tactics and the conduct of warfare, fundamentally altering the dynamics of battles and the nature of armies. As early as the first millennium BCE, mounted warriors began to emerge as a formidable force on the battlefield, leveraging the speed, mobility, and height advantage offered by horses. This development not only changed how battles were fought but also influenced the sociopolitical structures of various civilizations.

The Horse as a Military Asset

Horses provided distinct advantages in warfare. Firstly, their speed allowed cavalry units to execute rapid maneuvers that foot soldiers could not match. This enabled them to flank enemy formations, retreat swiftly when needed, and pursue fleeing foes with relentless efficiency. The psychological impact of cavalry charges could instill fear in enemy troops, often leading to a breakdown in morale before a battle even commenced.

Moreover, the height advantage conferred by being mounted allowed cavalrymen to observe the battlefield from a superior vantage point. This observation capability facilitated better strategic planning and execution during engagements. Cavalry units could scout ahead, gather intelligence on enemy positions, and relay vital information back to commanders, enhancing the overall effectiveness of military strategies.

Evolution of Tactics

The rise of cavalry necessitated a shift in battlefield tactics. Traditional linear formations, which had been effective for infantry combat, became less viable against mobile horsemen. As a result, armies began to adopt more adaptive strategies that incorporated the strengths of cavalry. The use of cavalry as a striking force allowed for the implementation of tactics such as the "hit-and-run," where cavalry would strike quickly and retreat before the enemy could effectively respond.

Additionally, the integration of cavalry into larger military formations became commonplace. For instance, the ancient Greeks and Romans effectively utilized cavalry to support their infantry, creating a combined-arms approach that maximized the strengths of both mounted and foot soldiers. The renowned Macedonian phalanx under Alexander the Great is a prime example of how cavalry could complement infantry, with cavalry executing flanking maneuvers that caught enemies off guard, leading to decisive victories.

Cultural and Political Implications

The prominence of cavalry in warfare also had significant cultural and political ramifications. In many societies, the ability to own and maintain horses became a symbol of status and power. Warrior elites often emerged as a distinct class, with their wealth tied to their ability to field cavalry forces. This social stratification fostered loyalty among cavalrymen, who were often rewarded with land and titles for their military service.

As cavalry units gained prominence, they influenced the organization of armies and the nature of military leadership. Commanders often needed to be skilled horsemen themselves, and the ability to lead cavalry effectively became a mark of an accomplished military leader. The societal reverence for cavalrymen is reflected in the chivalric codes that emerged in medieval Europe, where knighthood and mounted combat became synonymous with noble virtues and martial prowess.

Conclusion

The rise of cavalry fundamentally reshaped the landscape of warfare. By harnessing the speed and agility of horses, armies could execute new tactics that placed a premium on mobility and rapid engagement. This shift not only impacted military strategies but also shaped societal structures, creating a lasting legacy that would influence the organization of armies and the nature of power for centuries to come. As the role of mounted warriors evolved, their impact on warfare and society underscored the enduring significance of cavalry in the annals of military history.

The Role of Iron in Defensive Technologies

The transition from bronze to iron during the Iron Age marked a pivotal moment in the history of weaponry and defensive technologies. This period, roughly spanning from 1200 BCE to 600

CE, not only witnessed the mass production of iron tools and weapons but also led to significant advancements in armor and fortifications that fundamentally altered the dynamics of warfare and societal structures.

Iron, being more abundant and less costly than bronze, allowed for the widespread availability of stronger materials. The hardness of iron, when properly smelted and forged, enabled the creation of armor that provided superior protection for soldiers in combat. The development of iron armor included the introduction of mail, or chain armor, which consisted of interlinked metal rings. This design offered flexibility and enhanced mobility while maintaining a high degree of defense against slashing weapons. Unlike earlier bronze armor, which was typically rigid and heavy, iron mail was lighter and allowed for greater agility on the battlefield.

Additionally, iron plates began to be used to create more substantial defensive gear, such as the cuirass — a breastplate that protected the torso. The use of iron in armor not only improved individual soldier safety but also influenced the overall tactics of warfare. Armies equipped with iron armor could engage in more aggressive strategies, knowing that their troops had better protection against enemy attacks. This shift compelled opposing forces to innovate their weaponry, leading to the development of weapons specifically designed to penetrate iron armor.

The enhancements in personal armor were paralleled by advancements in fortifications. Iron played a critical role in the construction of defensive structures, such as gates and walls. As cities grew and became more complex, the need for robust defenses against invasions became apparent. Iron reinforcements were incorporated into wooden gates, making them more resilient against battering rams and other siege weapons. The introduction of iron spikes and caltrops provided additional layers of defense against attackers attempting to breach fortifications.

The architectural strategies employed in fortifications evolved as well, with iron allowing for the creation of more intricate designs. Iron was used to strengthen the structural integrity of walls, enabling them to withstand greater forces during sieges. This led to the construction of towering ramparts and fortified castles that dominated the landscape and provided strategic advantages in both defense and military logistics.

Moreover, the use of iron in fortifications influenced the development of siege weaponry. As armies adapted to fortified positions, they began to devise new methods for breaching defenses. The introduction of powerful siege engines, such as the trebuchet and later the cannon, was a direct response to the advancements in defensive technologies that iron enabled. These weapons were designed to counter the formidable iron-reinforced walls and gates of fortified cities, highlighting the ongoing arms race between offense and defense.

The impact of iron on defensive technologies extended beyond the battlefield. The presence of fortified cities equipped with iron defenses shaped political landscapes, allowing certain regions to maintain power and control over surrounding territories. These fortified strongholds became centers of trade and commerce, significantly contributing to the economic stability of civilizations. The protection offered by iron armor and fortifications thus not only influenced military tactics but also had broader implications for societal organization and the balance of power in ancient and medieval contexts.

In conclusion, the role of iron in the development of armor and fortifications was transformative. It catalyzed a shift in military strategy, enhanced personal protection for soldiers, and reinforced the structures that protected communities. The advancements in iron technology during the Iron Age set the stage for the evolution of warfare, influencing both the tactics of combat and the architecture of defense that would be utilized for centuries to come.

The Influence of Iron Weaponry on Ancient Empires

The transition from bronze to iron weaponry marked a significant turning point in the dynamics of ancient warfare and the rise and fall of empires. This transition, often referred to as the Iron Age, began around 1200 BCE in regions such as the Near East and later swept across Europe and Asia. The introduction of iron weapons not only enhanced military effectiveness but also reshaped social structures, economies, and political power dynamics within and between ancient civilizations.

Iron weaponry was characterized by its superior strength and availability compared to bronze. Iron ore was more abundant and easier to source than the copper and tin required for bronze. This accessibility meant that more societies could produce weapons, thus democratizing military power. As a result, states and tribes that could harness ironworking technology gained a decisive edge in conflicts. Increased production capabilities allowed for larger armies to be equipped with weapons that were not only more durable but also sharper and capable of inflicting greater damage.

One of the most notable advantages of iron weaponry was the evolution of the sword. The transition from bronze to iron swords allowed for longer, more versatile blades that were effective in close combat. Empires such as the Assyrians and later the Romans capitalized on this development, creating formidable infantry that could engage effectively in battle. The Roman legions, equipped with iron gladii (short swords), became renowned for their discipline and effectiveness, enabling Rome to expand its territory extensively.

In addition to swords, the development of iron-tipped spears and arrowheads revolutionized ranged combat. Armies equipped with iron weapons could engage enemies at greater distances with increased lethality. The ability to manufacture a higher volume of these weapons meant that armies could also sustain prolonged engagements, ultimately leading to a shift in military strategy and tactics. This shift contributed to the rise of powerful empires that could project force over vast territories.

The influence of iron weaponry also extended to the development of cavalry, which became a vital component of ancient armies. Iron stirrups and horse harnesses improved the effectiveness of mounted troops, allowing for greater maneuverability and shock tactics in battle. Empires like the Persians leveraged these advancements, creating highly mobile forces that could strike swiftly and decisively. The integration of cavalry into military strategies transformed the landscape of warfare and contributed significantly to the expansion and dominance of these empires.

However, the proliferation of iron weaponry also had profound implications for the political landscape of ancient societies. As iron weapons became more widely available, power began to shift from established aristocracies to a broader warrior class. The rise of heavily armed infantry and cavalry led to changes in social hierarchies, often empowering those who could afford to equip themselves with iron arms. This shift sometimes resulted in social unrest and challenges to existing power structures, as new military leaders emerged from the ranks of the common population.

Furthermore, the widespread availability of iron weapons contributed to the decline of some empires. As various tribes and groups gained access to iron technology, they could challenge established powers more effectively. The Huns, for instance, utilized iron weaponry to great effect against the Roman Empire, contributing to its eventual decline. The ability of smaller groups to field effective military forces against larger empires underscored the disruptive potential of iron weaponry in the ancient world.

In conclusion, iron weaponry was a transformative force in ancient empires. It not only enhanced military capabilities, allowing for the rise of powerful armies and the expansion of territories but also reshaped social structures and political hierarchies. As iron weapons became widespread, they played a crucial role in both the ascent and the decline of empires, highlighting the complex interplay between technology, warfare, and societal change in the ancient world.

Chapter 4

Classical Warfare and Weaponry

The Phalanx and Hoplite Warfare

In classical Greece, the evolution of warfare was profoundly influenced by the introduction of the phalanx formation and the use of hoplite soldiers. This shift not only transformed military tactics but also had lasting impacts on Greek society and its political landscape. The phalanx, characterized by a dense arrangement of heavily armed infantry, became the dominant military formation of the time, relying heavily on the specific weaponry and strategic organization of its soldiers.

The Hoplite Soldier

The hoplite was a citizen-soldier of ancient Greece, typically belonging to the middle class. Equipped with a range of weapons and armor, the hoplite was primarily distinguished by a large round shield known as the "hoplon," a helmet, a breastplate, and a spear measuring roughly 8 to 10 feet in length, referred to as a "doru." Additionally, many hoplites carried a short sword, known as a "xiphos," for close combat. The heavy armor and equipment of the hoplite, while cumbersome, provided significant protection and allowed them to engage effectively in hand-to-hand combat.

The Phalanx Formation

The phalanx formation was a tightly packed arrangement of hoplites, typically eight to twelve ranks deep. Each soldier stood shoulder-to-shoulder with the man to his left, creating a wall of shields that provided mutual protection. The front line was composed of the most experienced and heavily armored soldiers, while the ranks behind were filled with less experienced troops. This structure was not only effective in defending against enemy attacks but also allowed for a powerful offensive capability when the formation advanced toward the enemy.

One of the key advantages of the phalanx was its ability to maintain cohesion and discipline. The soldiers relied on each other for support, and any break in formation could lead to disaster. This reliance fostered a sense of camaraderie and collective responsibility among the hoplites, which was crucial in the heat of battle. Commanders, often from the ranks of the aristocracy, trained their troops to maintain formation under pressure, emphasizing the importance of discipline and unity.

Tactical Advantages and Challenges

The phalanx was particularly effective in open terrain, where its organization could be fully utilized. The sheer weight of the advancing hoplites, combined with the overlapping shields, created an almost impenetrable barrier that could push through enemy lines. The spear, thrusting forward with the weight of multiple ranks, could inflict devastating damage on opposing forces.

However, the phalanx also had its limitations. Its effectiveness diminished in rough or uneven terrain, where the tightly packed formation could become disorganized. Additionally, the reliance on frontal assaults made the phalanx vulnerable to flanking maneuvers. Opposing armies, such as the Persians, began to adapt by employing cavalry and archers that could exploit these weaknesses.

The Evolution of Warfare

The prominence of the phalanx and hoplite warfare marked a significant shift in ancient Greek military strategy. It democratized the military by allowing citizens to participate in warfare, thus connecting military service to civic identity. The hoplite's role extended beyond the battlefield, influencing the political landscape of city-states. As hoplites gained prominence, they often demanded greater political rights and representation, leading to shifts in governance, including the rise of democracy in Athens.

In conclusion, the phalanx and hoplite warfare represented a transformative period in classical Greece, characterized by collective military action, the rise of citizen-soldiers, and the interplay between military capability and political power. The tactics employed in these formations set the stage for future developments in warfare, influencing not only Greek military history but also the broader trajectory of Western military strategy.

The Roman Legion

The Roman Legion stands as one of the most effective military forces in history, renowned for its innovative weapons, sophisticated tactics, and disciplined organization. The evolution of Roman military strategy was instrumental in the expansion and consolidation of the Roman Empire, allowing it to dominate the ancient world for centuries.

At the heart of the Roman military was the legion, a flexible unit typically comprising about 4,500 to 6,000 soldiers. The legion was divided into smaller groups known as centuries and maniples, allowing for adaptability in various combat situations. This structure enabled the Romans to execute complex maneuvers on the battlefield, a feature that set them apart from many of their contemporaries, who relied on less organized formations.

One of the key innovations of the Roman Legion was its weaponry. The primary infantry weapon was the gladius, a short sword designed for close combat. The gladius, with its double-edged blade, was effective for thrusting attacks, allowing soldiers to engage enemies in tight formations. This was complemented by the pilum, a throwing spear that could penetrate enemy shields and armor, disrupting formations before the infantry closed in for melee. The pilum's design allowed it to bend upon impact, preventing enemies from throwing it back. This combination of ranged and close-quarters weaponry was critical in maintaining the tactical advantage in battle.

The Romans also utilized scutums, large rectangular shields that provided extensive protection and were often used in a formation known as the testudo or "tortoise." In this formation, soldiers would align their shields to form a protective barrier, with those in the front using their shields to create a wall and those in the rear and above forming a roof against projectiles. This tactic not only protected the legionaries from enemy missiles but also allowed them to advance toward fortified positions effectively.

Tactics played a crucial role in the success of the Roman Legion. The Romans favored a methodical approach to warfare, often relying on formations that maximized their strengths while minimizing vulnerabilities. The manipular formation allowed for greater flexibility than the phalanx used by Greek armies, enabling the Romans to maneuver effectively across various terrains. In open battles, the ability to shift formations rapidly allowed them to exploit weaknesses in enemy lines, often leading to decisive victories.

The Roman military was also characterized by its engineering capabilities. The construction of fortifications, siege engines, and roads facilitated not only military campaigns but also the movement of troops and supplies. The use of siege towers, battering rams, and catapults allowed Roman forces to breach enemy fortifications and effectively conduct siege warfare. The engineering prowess of the Romans ensured that they could lay siege to cities with the means to maintain prolonged assaults, which was crucial in their expansionist campaigns.

Moreover, the integration of auxiliary forces—non-citizen troops who provided additional cavalry and specialized infantry—enhanced the legions' capabilities. These auxiliaries, often skilled in different types of warfare, contributed to the versatility of the Roman military, allowing them to adapt to various combat scenarios encountered throughout the diverse landscapes of the Empire.

In conclusion, the Roman Legion's innovations in weapons and tactics were fundamental to its dominance over the ancient world. The effective combination of disciplined organization, advanced weaponry, and tactical flexibility enabled the Romans to conquer and maintain vast territories. Their military legacy not only influenced subsequent generations of military leaders but also shaped the course of history, establishing principles of warfare that remain relevant today.

Siege Warfare in the Classical World

Siege warfare in the Classical world represented a sophisticated evolution of military strategy and technology, reflecting the growing complexity of warfare as city-states and empires sought to dominate their rivals. The period, stretching from approximately the 8th century BCE to the fall of the Western Roman Empire in the 5th century CE, witnessed significant advancements in siege technology and tactics that fundamentally altered the dynamics of conflict.

The Importance of Siege Warfare

Sieges were often the decisive element in warfare during this era, as fortified cities served as critical strongholds for political power and economic resources. Commanding a fortified city allowed a state to control trade routes, defend territory, and exert influence over surrounding regions. Consequently, besieging an enemy stronghold was typically a strategic priority, compelling military leaders to develop specialized tactics and technologies to breach these defenses.

Innovations in Siege Weapons

The Classical world saw the invention and refinement of several advanced siege weapons, each designed to counter different aspects of fortifications. The most notable developments included:

1. The Battering Ram: One of the earliest and most effective siege weapons, the battering ram was a heavy wooden beam, often reinforced with metal, that was swung against the gates or walls of a besieged city. With the addition of protective covers, soldiers could operate the ram while minimizing exposure to enemy projectiles, thereby increasing its effectiveness.

2. Siege Ladders and Towers: To overcome high walls, armies utilized ladders and constructed siege towers. Ladders allowed infantry to scale walls quickly, while siege towers, often wheeled and covered, provided a mobile platform from which soldiers could assault the battlements. These towers could be equipped with archers and other missile troops, allowing for a multifaceted attack on fortifications.

3. The Catapult: Perhaps the most significant advancement in siege technology was the development of the catapult. Various types, such as the torsion catapult and the ballista, were engineered to hurl large projectiles—rocks, incendiaries, or even dead animals—over or into city walls. This form of artillery increased the range and lethality of siege operations, allowing attackers to weaken defenses from a distance.

4. The Trebuchet: Emerging later in the Classical period, the trebuchet represented a significant leap in siege technology. Using a counterweight mechanism, it could launch larger projectiles over greater distances with improved accuracy. The introduction of the trebuchet marked a transition in siege warfare, as its capability to cause widespread destruction changed how defenders approached fortifications.

Tactics of Siege Warfare

The tactics employed during sieges were as crucial as the weapons themselves. Classical military leaders developed comprehensive strategies that included:

- **Blockade and Starvation:** A common tactic involved surrounding a city to cut off supplies and reinforcements, effectively starving the defenders into submission. This approach often proved effective, as prolonged sieges could lead to desperation and capitulation without the need for direct assault.

- **Psychological Warfare:** Psychological tactics, including the use of propaganda and displays of overwhelming force, were employed to demoralize defenders. The sight of advanced siege engines or the sounds of battering rams could instill fear and lead to surrender.

- **Coordinated Assaults:** Effective sieges often involved coordinated attacks on multiple fronts, stretching the defenders' resources thin and creating opportunities for breaches. This required meticulous planning and execution, showcasing the military acumen of leaders like Alexander the Great and Roman generals.

Conclusion

Siege warfare in the Classical world was characterized by an intricate interplay between technological innovation and tactical evolution. As cities fortified themselves against increasingly sophisticated siege weapons, military leaders adapted their strategies accordingly, leading to a cycle of innovation in both offense and defense. The legacy of these developments not only shaped the outcomes of individual conflicts but also laid the groundwork for the future of military strategy and technology in subsequent eras. The lessons learned from siege warfare during this period continue to resonate in modern military doctrine, highlighting the enduring significance of these ancient practices.

Naval Warfare

Naval warfare in the classical era represents a pivotal chapter in the evolution of military strategy, technology, and commerce. Prior to the advent of sophisticated naval vessels, maritime engagements were rudimentary and often limited to coastal skirmishes. However, with the development of the trireme—an advanced warship that emerged around the 5th century BCE—naval conflict transformed dramatically, significantly impacting the balance of power in the ancient Mediterranean world.

The trireme was a sleek, fast vessel characterized by its three tiers of oars, manned by skilled rowers, a design that allowed for unprecedented speed and maneuverability. This innovation was crucial in naval battles, enabling fleets to outpace and outmaneuver their enemies. The trireme's design emphasized both offensive and defensive capabilities, making it a formidable tool in warfare. It was equipped with a bronze ram at the prow, allowing it to strike enemy ships with devastating force, often leading to the sinking or incapacitation of foes before they could retaliate.

The significance of the trireme was most evident during the Persian Wars, particularly in the Battle of Salamis in 480 BCE. This decisive naval engagement, in which the Greek city-states united against the invading Persian forces, showcased the tactical prowess of trireme crews. The narrow straits of Salamis favored the maneuverability of the Greek fleet, enabling them to exploit their superior tactics against a larger Persian force. The victory not only secured Greek independence but also demonstrated the importance of naval power in shaping the outcomes of larger conflicts.

As naval warfare evolved, so did the design and technology of ships. Following the trireme, the development of larger ships, such as the quinquereme—which had five rows of oars—allowed for greater firepower and troop transport. These ships became central to the strategies of powerful empires, including the Macedonian and Roman fleets, which utilized them to project power across vast distances, control trade routes, and establish dominance over rival states.

The Roman Navy, particularly during the Punic Wars against Carthage, exemplified the evolution of naval warfare. Rome adopted a strategy that combined the use of smaller, agile vessels with the integration of land forces to maximize their tactical advantages. The introduction of the corvus—a boarding device that allowed Roman soldiers to board enemy ships—illustrated a shift in naval tactics, emphasizing hand-to-hand combat rather than solely relying on ramming and sinking enemy vessels. This adaptation allowed Rome to capitalize on its superior infantry, transforming naval engagements into extensions of land battles.

Beyond the trireme and its successors, naval warfare in classical antiquity also involved the development of naval bases and the establishment of supply lines. Control of key maritime chokepoints became essential for maintaining dominance in the region. For instance, the strategic importance of the Strait of Gibraltar and the Aegean Sea underscored the need for powerful naval forces to protect trade routes and ensure the flow of resources.

The advancement of naval technology during this period set the stage for future developments in maritime warfare. Innovations such as improved sail designs, navigation techniques, and communication methods would influence naval engagements for centuries to come. Moreover, the legacy of classical naval warfare, exemplified by the trireme, is seen in the continued emphasis on speed, maneuverability, and strategic positioning in modern naval doctrines.

In conclusion, the role of ships and naval technology in classical conflicts cannot be overstated. The trireme and its successors were not merely vessels of war; they were instruments of strategy that shaped the political landscape of the ancient world. The mastery of naval warfare allowed states to project power beyond their borders, control vital trade routes, and secure their dominance in a competitive geopolitical environment. The innovations and strategies developed during this era laid the groundwork for the future of naval combat, influencing maritime military practices for generations to follow.

Gladiators and Arena Weapons

The spectacle of gladiatorial combat was a defining aspect of Roman culture, serving not only as a form of public entertainment but also as a means of demonstrating power, bravery, and the martial prowess of Rome. The arena, typically a grand structure like the Colosseum, became the stage for these brutal contests, where gladiators wielded an array of specialized weapons designed for both lethality and dramatic effect. Understanding the types of weapons used in these combats provides insight into the nature of gladiatorial games and their significance in Roman society.

Types of Gladiators and Their Weapons

Gladiators were often categorized by their fighting style and the weapons they carried, with each type playing a specific role in the arena. The most recognized categories include the Murmillo, Thraex, and Secutor:

1. Murmillo: This type of gladiator was typically equipped with a short sword called a gladius, which was effective in close combat. Murmillos also carried a rectangular shield known as a scutum, which offered substantial protection. Their armor often included a helmet adorned with distinctive fish motifs, symbolizing their name, derived from the Latin word for 'fish.'

2. Thraex: The Thracian gladiator wielded a sica, a curved sword ideal for slashing attacks, and usually carried a small shield. The Thraex was often depicted with a crested helmet and a protective arm guard, allowing for both mobility and defense. Their fighting style emphasized agility and the ability to maneuver around opponents.

3. Secutor: This gladiator was designed to combat the Thraex and other agile foes. Armed with a gladius and a large shield, the Secutor wore a helmet that featured small eye openings, providing limited visibility but enhancing protection. The Secutor's strategy usually involved enduring the initial flurry of attacks before launching a powerful counterstrike.

Arena Weapons and Their Symbolism

The weapons used in gladiatorial combat were not merely instruments of violence; they also carried significant symbolic weight. The gladius, for instance, became synonymous with Roman military power, representing both the might of the legions and the valor of the gladiators who wielded it. The act of fighting with such weapons allowed gladiators to embody the Roman ideals of courage, honor, and sacrifice.

In addition to swords and shields, other weapons included the trident and net used by the Retiarius, a gladiator who fought with a unique strategy that involved entangling his opponent before delivering a fatal blow with his trident. The Retiarius's distinctive weaponry highlighted the diverse fighting styles in the arena and catered to the crowd's desire for varied combat scenarios.

The Role of Gladiatorial Combat in Society

Gladiatorial games served multiple purposes beyond mere entertainment. They were a means for emperors and wealthy sponsors to showcase their power and generosity, often commemorating military victories or significant events. The games also provided a platform for social commentary, as the outcomes of battles could reflect broader themes of justice, morality, and fate.

Moreover, the weapons and armor of gladiators were often decorated or customized to reflect the personality and background of the fighter, further enhancing their role as public figures. The narratives surrounding these weapons contributed to the spectacle of the games, allowing spectators to engage emotionally with the combatants.

Conclusion

The weapons used by gladiators in ancient Rome were integral to the culture of spectacle and violence that characterized the era. From the gladius to the sica, each weapon symbolized not only the martial skills of the gladiators but also the values of Roman society as a whole. As a reflection of power dynamics, social structure, and cultural identity, gladiatorial weaponry continues to captivate historians and enthusiasts alike, revealing the complexity of ancient Roman entertainment and its lasting legacy.

Chapter 5

Medieval Weaponry

The Sword in the Middle Ages

The sword, often considered the quintessential weapon of the medieval period, emerged as a powerful symbol of chivalry, honor, and martial prowess during an era characterized by feudalism and knightly culture. As a direct evolution from earlier bladed weapons, the medieval sword's design and significance underwent notable transformations, reflecting both technological advancements and the sociopolitical landscape of the time.

Evolution of the Sword

By the early Middle Ages, the sword had transitioned from the broad, heavy blades of the Viking Age to more refined designs, such as the arming sword, which featured a straight, double-edged blade and a crossguard. This evolution paralleled changes in combat tactics, where the need for agility and versatility became paramount. The arming sword was typically around 30 to 40 inches long, allowing knights to wield it effectively both on foot and horseback. As the late Middle Ages approached, the longsword gained popularity, with its longer blade enabling thrusting attacks and more complex fighting techniques, such as those codified in the martial arts treatises of the period.

Symbol of Chivalry

The sword was not merely a weapon; it was a potent symbol of the ideals of chivalry that defined medieval knighthood. Chivalry encompassed a code of conduct that emphasized virtues such as bravery, loyalty, honor, and the protection of the weak. The act of receiving a sword was often tied to the ceremony of knighthood, where young squires were dubbed knights in elaborate rituals that included the conferral of a sword. This moment symbolized the knight's commitment to uphold the moral and ethical standards of their class, making the sword a representation of their duty to society.

Knights adorned their swords with intricate designs, engravings, and heraldic motifs, further enhancing their symbolic value. The sword was often passed down through generations, becoming a family heirloom that carried the legacy of valor and honor associated with its previous owners. In this context, the sword transcended its practical use as a weapon and became an emblem of identity and social status within the feudal hierarchy.

Combat and Warfare

In the context of warfare, the sword's role was multifaceted. While it was the weapon of choice for close combat, knights were also trained in various other weapons and techniques, including lance, polearm, and hand-to-hand combat. The sword was particularly significant during mounted combat, where a knight's ability to wield their weapon effectively from horseback could determine the outcome of battles. As warfare evolved, so too did the tactics associated with swordsmanship. The rise of heavily armored knights necessitated the development of specialized techniques to penetrate armor, leading to the emergence of the longsword and other bladed weapons designed for versatility against both armored and unarmored foes.

Moreover, the prominence of the sword in medieval warfare was mirrored in the formation of military orders, such as the Knights Templar and the Knights Hospitaller, whose members were renowned for their martial skills and commitment to their cause. These orders not only wielded swords in battle but also used them as tools of religious and political power, further embedding the sword into the very fabric of medieval society.

Conclusion

In conclusion, the sword in the Middle Ages served as more than just a tool of war; it was a vital component of the knightly identity and the chivalric code. As a weapon, it underwent significant evolution, adapting to the changing nature of combat while remaining a steadfast symbol of honor and valor. Its legacy continues to resonate, reminding us of a time when the sword was the ultimate embodiment of the knight's duty, power, and prestige in a world shaped by warfare and the pursuit of ideals.

The Longbow and the Crossbow

The medieval period witnessed a significant evolution in ranged weaponry, exemplified by the longbow and the crossbow. These weapons not only transformed combat dynamics but also influenced the very fabric of medieval society, shaping military tactics, social hierarchies, and the outcomes of key battles.

The Longbow: Mastery of Range and Skill

The longbow, a formidable weapon made typically from yew, ash, or elm, emerged prominently in the late Middle Ages, particularly within England. Standing at an impressive height of six feet or more, the longbow offered a range that far surpassed that of earlier ranged weapons like the shortbow. Capable of shooting arrows at distances exceeding 200 yards, the longbow allowed archers to engage enemies from a safe distance, a tactical advantage that significantly altered battlefield strategy.

A hallmark of the longbow was not merely its range but also the skill required to wield it effectively. Proficiency demanded extensive training, often starting from a young age. This commitment to mastering the longbow was evident in the English military, where archery became a crucial aspect of military training. The famous English victories at the Battle of Crécy (1346) and the Battle of Agincourt (1415) showcased the longbow's devastating impact, as English archers decimated French forces with a relentless barrage of arrows. These battles underscored the longbow's ability to penetrate armor, making it a decisive factor in medieval warfare.

The Crossbow: Mechanized Precision

In contrast to the longbow, the crossbow represented a different approach to ranged combat. Its design, which utilized a horizontal bow mounted on a stock, allowed for a mechanical advantage. The crossbow was easier to use for those lacking the years of training required for the longbow; it required less upper body strength and could be operated effectively by soldiers of varying physical capabilities. This accessibility led to its widespread adoption across Europe, especially among infantry units.

The crossbow's most significant advantage lay in its power and precision. Equipped with a heavier draw weight, crossbows could shoot bolts capable of piercing armor that the longbow's arrows might struggle to penetrate. This made the crossbow a preferred choice in sieges and against heavily armored knights, further shifting the power dynamics on the battlefield. However, the crossbow did have its drawbacks: the time needed to reload was considerably longer than that of the longbow, which necessitated strategic deployment on the battlefield.

Impact on Warfare and Society

The emergence of these ranged weapons not only revolutionized military tactics but also had broader societal implications. The longbow and crossbow enabled the rise of a more diverse range of military personnel. While the feudal system had largely relied on heavily armored knights, the effective use of these ranged weapons allowed for the inclusion of common soldiers, particularly archers, in military campaigns. The English longbowmen became celebrated figures, and their contributions shifted perceptions regarding social status and military prowess.

Moreover, the proliferation of these weapons contributed to significant changes in fortification design. Castles and fortified towns began to incorporate features designed to counter the effects of long-range archery and crossbow fire. This evolution in defensive architecture underscored an ongoing arms race between attackers and defenders, prompting continuous innovation.

Conclusion

In conclusion, the longbow and crossbow epitomized the evolution of ranged weaponry in medieval Europe, each fulfilling distinct roles in combat while reshaping military and social structures. The longbow's emphasis on skill and range contrasted with the crossbow's mechanized power and accessibility, together marking a transformative period in warfare. Their influence extended beyond the battlefield, fostering a new class of soldiers and inspiring changes in military strategy and societal norms that would resonate throughout the ages.

The Rise of Heavy Cavalry

The medieval period, often characterized by the feudal system and a highly stratified society, witnessed significant transformations in warfare, particularly with the emergence of heavy cavalry. Mounted knights became the epitome of military might and social prestige, fundamentally altering the dynamics of the battlefield from the 9th to the 15th centuries. This section explores the factors leading to the rise of heavy cavalry, the tactical advantages it offered, and its broader implications for medieval society.

Origins and Evolution

The origins of heavy cavalry can be traced back to the Carolingian Empire in the 8th century, where Charlemagne employed mounted warriors as a vital component of his military strategy. Initially, these cavalrymen were equipped with rudimentary armor and weaponry, primarily relying on speed and mobility. However, as warfare evolved, so did the need for better protection and offensive capabilities. By the 11th century, advancements in metallurgy allowed for the production of heavier armor and more effective weapons, leading to the emergence of the fully armored knight—an elite warrior class characterized by their distinctive plate armor, large shields, and lances.

The Tactical Advantages of Heavy Cavalry

The tactical advantages of heavy cavalry were manifold. Firstly, the sheer physical presence of heavily armored knights on horseback instilled fear in opposing forces. The charge of a cavalry unit, spearheaded by knights, could break enemy lines and disrupt formations, leading to psychological advantages on the battlefield. Knights were trained to fight in close formation, utilizing their lances for powerful charges, and their swords for close combat, creating a formidable offensive force.

Moreover, the mobility of heavy cavalry allowed for rapid maneuvers on the battlefield. Unlike infantry, which was often bogged down by terrain or encumbered by heavy shields and armor, cavalry could quickly reposition to exploit weaknesses in enemy lines or to retreat and regroup when necessary. This mobility was particularly advantageous in the context of feudal warfare, where battles often revolved around controlling key territories and resources.

Social and Political Implications

The rise of heavy cavalry was not only a military phenomenon but also a social and political one. Knights, as the mounted elite, became central figures in the feudal hierarchy. Their status was often tied to land ownership; lords granted fiefs to knights in exchange for military service, solidifying the bond between landholding and military obligation. This relationship reinforced the feudal system, as the loyalty of knights was paramount to the stability of their lords' domains.

Additionally, the chivalric code—an unwritten set of ethical guidelines governing knightly conduct—emerged during this time, further elevating the social standing of knights. The ideals of bravery, honor, and loyalty not only shaped the behavior of knights in battle but also influenced the culture of the medieval nobility. Tournaments and jousts became popular spectacles, reinforcing the image of the knight as both a warrior and a gentleman, and allowing knights to showcase their martial prowess.

Decline of Heavy Cavalry
Despite their dominance, the age of heavy cavalry began to wane toward the late medieval period. Several factors contributed to this decline, including the rise of more effective infantry tactics, the increased use of long-range weaponry such as the longbow, and the advent of gunpowder technology. These developments diminished the effectiveness of heavily armored knights, leading to a reevaluation of military strategies.

In conclusion, the rise of heavy cavalry during the medieval period significantly shaped the nature of warfare and the social structures of the time. The mounted knight, with their formidable presence and tactical advantages, embodied the militaristic and chivalric ideals of the age. While their dominance eventually gave way to new forms of warfare, the legacy of heavy cavalry remains a defining feature of medieval history, influencing military tactics and social hierarchies for centuries to come.

Siege Engines
Siege engines represent a pivotal evolution in the art of warfare, particularly during the medieval period when the dynamics of combat shifted dramatically with the introduction of more sophisticated siege technologies. As castles and fortified cities became increasingly prevalent, the need for effective methods to breach these formidable defenses became paramount. This led to the development of various siege engines, most notably the trebuchet and the cannon, which played crucial roles in determining the outcomes of conflicts.

The Trebuchet: A Masterpiece of Leverage
Among the earliest and most effective siege engines was the trebuchet, a counterweight-powered throwing machine that emerged in Europe around the 12th century. Its design was revolutionary, utilizing the principles of leverage to hurl projectiles over formidable

walls. The trebuchet's capability to launch heavy stones, incendiary devices, and even diseased corpses aimed to demoralize defenders and breach the walls of castles.

Trebuchets were highly effective due to their range and the weight of their projectiles, which could weigh up to 300 pounds. These machines could be constructed relatively quickly using local materials, making them accessible to besieging armies. The introduction of the trebuchet not only changed siege warfare but also influenced the architectural designs of castles, prompting builders to create stronger, higher, and more complex fortifications.

The Transition to Cannons

As the medieval period progressed, the invention of gunpowder in the 9th century in China eventually made its way to Europe, setting the stage for a revolutionary change in siege warfare. By the late 14th and early 15th centuries, the cannon emerged as a formidable siege engine, representing a transition from mechanical to explosive power.

Cannons offered several advantages over traditional siege engines like trebuchets. They could fire a variety of projectiles, including stone balls, iron cannonballs, and explosive shells, at greater speeds and with greater impact. The psychological effect of cannon fire was also significant; the sound and destruction caused by cannon fire could demoralize defenders more effectively than the hurling of stones.

The Development of Fortifications

The rise of cannons necessitated a corresponding evolution in fortification design. Castles and city walls that had once been effective against siege engines like trebuchets needed to be adapted to withstand cannon fire. This led to the development of thicker walls, angled bastions, and lower profiles, which were more resistant to the destructive power of cannons.

Additionally, the introduction of gunpowder artillery led to the construction of star forts and trace italienne designs, which maximized defensive capabilities while allowing for more effective counter-battery fire against besieging forces. This shift in military architecture was as influential as the siege engines themselves, illustrating the interconnected evolution of offense and defense in medieval warfare.

The Impact on Warfare and Society

The advancements in siege technology had profound implications not only for military tactics but also for the political landscape of Europe. The ability to effectively besiege and capture fortified locations contributed to the centralization of power as monarchs and warlords sought to expand their territories. The fall of key strongholds often led to significant shifts in power dynamics, with the victors often consolidating control over larger regions.

Moreover, the development and deployment of siege engines like trebuchets and cannons underscored the increasingly professional nature of warfare. As these technologies became more complex, the need for skilled operators and engineers grew, leading to the emergence of specialized military roles and a more organized approach to warfare.

Conclusion

In conclusion, the evolution of siege engines from trebuchets to cannons marked a significant turning point in medieval warfare. These advancements dramatically altered the strategies employed in sieges and necessitated changes in fortification design, ultimately transforming the political and social landscape of the era. The historical significance of these technologies extends beyond the battlefield, reflecting broader themes of innovation, adaptation, and the ever-changing nature of conflict.

The Role of Castles and Fortifications

During the medieval period, the rise of castles and fortified structures played a pivotal role in shaping military strategies and the development of weaponry. These defensive architectures were not just mere residences for the nobility but complex military installations that served multiple functions, including protection against invasions, a base for military operations, and a display of power and prestige.

Evolution of Castle Design

The design and construction of castles evolved significantly from the early motte-and-bailey designs to the more sophisticated stone fortifications seen later in the medieval period. The motte-and-bailey castle, characterized by a raised earth mound (the motte) topped with a wooden or stone keep, and an enclosed courtyard (the bailey), provided a quick and effective means of defense against early medieval warfare. However, as siege technology advanced, the need for stronger, more durable structures became apparent.

By the 12th century, stone castles emerged, featuring thick walls, rounded towers, and defensive features such as arrow slits, murder holes, and drawbridges. These innovations were crucial in enhancing the castle's resilience against siege weapons such as trebuchets and battering rams. The evolution of castle design was a direct response to the changing nature of warfare, where the emphasis shifted from raiding to prolonged sieges.

Strategic Importance of Fortifications

Castles served as strategic points for controlling territory and regional power dynamics. Positioned on high ground or near vital resources like rivers and trade routes, they allowed lords to oversee their lands and exert influence over surrounding areas. In many cases, the presence of a castle could deter potential aggressors simply by showcasing military capability and readiness.

Moreover, castles acted as rallying points for local forces during conflicts. They provided a secure location for gathering troops, stockpiling weapons, and organizing defense against invaders. The fortified structure enabled lords to maintain their power and authority, as control over a castle often equated to control over the surrounding populace.

Influence on Weaponry and Military Tactics

The existence of castles and fortifications necessitated the development of specialized weaponry and tactics. As siege warfare became more prevalent, so did the creation of advanced siege engines. Trebuchets, catapults, and later, cannons, were designed specifically to breach the thick stone walls of castles. These weapons represented significant technological advancements and underscored the arms race between offensive and defensive military capabilities.

In response to the growing threat posed by these siege weapons, defenders adapted their strategies and armaments. The introduction of crossbows, longbows, and later gunpowder artillery allowed defenders to strike at besieging forces from a distance, making it increasingly difficult for attackers to approach the walls unscathed. The design of defensive structures also evolved to incorporate features that could withstand bombardment, such as thicker walls and angled bastions that could deflect projectiles.

Cultural and Psychological Impact

Beyond their military significance, castles also served a cultural function. They were symbols of feudal power and authority, often becoming the centers of local governance and justice. The presence of a formidable castle could instill fear and respect among the populace and potential adversaries alike. The psychological aspect of fortifications was as important as their physical defenses, shaping the behavior of enemies and allies during conflicts.

In conclusion, castles and fortifications were not merely passive structures; they actively shaped medieval military strategies and the evolution of weaponry. As centers of power, they influenced territorial control and regional politics while necessitating advancements in defense and siege technology. The interplay between castles and warfare exemplifies the dynamic relationship between military innovation and architectural development throughout medieval history.

Chapter 6

The Introduction of Gunpowder

The Invention of Gunpowder

The invention of gunpowder marked a pivotal moment in the history of warfare, fundamentally altering the landscape of military strategy and technology across the globe. Originating in China during the 9th century, gunpowder was initially concocted by alchemists searching for an elixir of immortality. Composed of saltpeter (potassium nitrate), charcoal, and sulfur, this explosive mixture transitioned from a mere curiosity to a revolutionary tool of war that would reshape the dynamics of conflict.

Gunpowder's introduction to military applications began in the 10th century, with the Chinese utilizing it in various weapons, such as fire arrows and primitive bombs. By the 13th century, the use of gunpowder had spread to the Middle East and Europe, primarily through the Mongol invasions, which facilitated cultural and technological exchange along the Silk Road. As the knowledge of gunpowder spread, armies began to experiment with its use in cannons and firearms. This transition from traditional melee combat, which relied heavily on swords and cavalry, to gunpowder-based warfare marked a significant shift in military tactics.

The impact of gunpowder on warfare was profound. First and foremost, it democratized the battlefield. Previously, warfare had been dominated by knights and elite warriors who relied on skill and physical prowess. With the introduction of firearms, a peasant with a musket could potentially kill a knight in armor from a distance, effectively leveling the playing field. This shift in power dynamics began to erode the feudal systems that had long governed European societies, as the necessity for heavily armored cavalry diminished in the face of the rapid-fire musket and cannon.

Gunpowder also transformed siege warfare. Fortifications that had stood for centuries could be breached with the devastating power of cannons. Castles and city walls became increasingly obsolete as artillery technology progressed. The introduction of heavy siege cannons allowed armies to lay siege to previously impregnable fortresses, significantly altering the strategies used in warfare. Battles that once relied on the valor of infantry and cavalry became determined by the efficiency of artillery and the tactical deployment of gunpowder.

Moreover, the development of gunpowder directly influenced naval warfare. The dawn of the age of sail saw the emergence of warships equipped with cannons, fundamentally changing naval tactics. The battle of the seas became less about boarding actions and more about long-range engagements, with ships designed to unleash devastating barrages. This evolution played a crucial role in establishing naval powers like Spain, Britain, and the Netherlands, who capitalized on their maritime strength to expand their empires.

The influence of gunpowder extended beyond the battlefield; it also had far-reaching implications for global politics and colonialism. As European powers sought to expand their empires, the technological superiority demonstrated through gunpowder weaponry allowed them to conquer vast territories and subjugate indigenous populations. The resulting colonial expansions often led to the establishment of trade networks that would reshape economies and societies worldwide.

In conclusion, the invention of gunpowder catalyzed a global shift in warfare, transforming military tactics, political structures, and the very nature of conflict. Its introduction marked the end of traditional forms of combat and the rise of a new era defined by firearms and artillery. The consequences of this transformation were felt not only in military engagements but also in the broader socio-political landscape, influencing the rise and fall of empires and the course of history itself. As we reflect on this pivotal development, it is clear that the discovery of gunpowder was not merely a technological advancement but a defining moment that reshaped human civilization.

Early Firearms

The advent of firearms marked a significant turning point in the history of weaponry, fundamentally transforming the nature of warfare and battlefield dynamics. This evolution began in the late Middle Ages, with the development of rudimentary firearms that laid the groundwork for more sophisticated weaponry in the centuries that followed.

The Birth of Firearms

The earliest form of firearm emerged around the 13th century, coinciding with the introduction of gunpowder to Europe from Asia. Initially, these weapons were simple tubes made of metal or wood, known as hand cannons. They were often crudely constructed, with a barrel that could be loaded with gunpowder and projectiles. The hand cannon was typically ignited with an open flame, requiring the user to hold the weapon steady while lighting it, making it cumbersome and dangerous.

These early firearms were primarily used in sieges and against fortifications, where their ability to breach walls offered a tactical advantage. However, the effectiveness of hand cannons was limited by their inaccuracy and slow reload times. As the technology of metallurgy improved, so too did the design and efficiency of these weapons.

The Development of Matchlocks

By the 15th century, the matchlock mechanism was developed, which revolutionized the use of firearms. This innovation involved a trigger mechanism that held a burning match cord, which ignited the gunpowder when the trigger was pulled. This significant advancement allowed soldiers to fire more quickly and accurately than with earlier hand cannons. The matchlock firearm became the first true personal firearm, leading to a shift in military tactics.

Matchlocks were simpler to operate than their predecessors, which contributed to their widespread use among infantry. As armies recognized the potential of firearms, they began to integrate them into their formations, fundamentally altering combat strategies. The ability to fire a projectile at a range significantly greater than that of traditional weapons like bows and crossbows provided infantry units with new offensive capabilities.

Tactical Implications

The integration of matchlocks into military units changed the face of battle. Armies began to develop formations that maximized the effectiveness of firearms. The introduction of units specifically trained in the use of matchlocks, known as arquebusiers, allowed for coordinated volleys of gunfire, creating a wall of bullets that could devastate enemy formations. This tactic was a precursor to modern infantry tactics, demonstrating a shift from individual combat to coordinated mass fire.

Moreover, the psychological impact of firearms cannot be understated. The noise, smoke, and power of gunfire contributed to a new level of fear on the battlefield. Traditional combatants, accustomed to facing swords and arrows, were often unprepared for the lethality of firearms. This psychological warfare played a crucial role in battles, as troops faced not only the physical threat of gunfire but also the demoralizing effect it had on their ranks.

Conclusion

The evolution from hand cannons to matchlocks marks a pivotal chapter in the history of weaponry. The development of firearms not only transformed military tactics and formations but also initiated a shift in the social dynamics of warfare. As firearms became more prevalent, they began to replace traditional weapons, signaling the decline of the knightly class and the rise of professional infantry. The innovations of this period laid the groundwork for further advancements in firearms technology, leading to the sophisticated weaponry that would dominate future conflicts. As such, the development of early firearms represented not just a technological leap, but a fundamental reorientation of how wars were fought and societies structured around military power.

Gunpowder Artillery

The advent of gunpowder in the 9th century, originating from China, marked a transformative period in military history, particularly in the realm of siege warfare. This innovation fundamentally altered the landscape of armed conflict, introducing new dynamics that would reshape the strategies, tactics, and technologies employed by armies across the globe.

Gunpowder, a mixture of saltpeter, charcoal, and sulfur, was first utilized in the form of simple explosive devices. However, it was not until the development of artillery that its true potential as a weapon of warfare was realized. The earliest forms of artillery were rudimentary cannon-like devices known as bombards, which emerged in Europe during the late 14th century. These early cannons were often made from wrought iron or bronze and were capable of launching projectiles over considerable distances, thereby challenging the long-standing dominance of traditional siege tactics.

The introduction of cannons revolutionized siege warfare in several key ways. Firstly, they significantly increased the destructive power that besieging forces could bring to bear against fortified structures. Previously, siege warfare relied heavily on manpower and tactics such as surrounding a city, cutting off supplies, or using siege towers and ladders to breach walls. The capability to launch heavy projectiles at fortifications allowed armies to breach walls with unprecedented efficiency. As a result, cities that had once seemed impregnable could be brought to their knees within days or even hours.

Mortars, another critical advancement in gunpowder artillery, played a pivotal role in this transformation. Unlike cannons, which fired projectiles along a relatively flat trajectory, mortars were designed to launch explosive shells at high angles. This capability allowed them to target not only the walls of fortifications but also the interiors of castles and fortified cities, inflicting damage on troops and supplies within. The ability to drop explosive shells over walls and into courtyards fundamentally changed how defenders approached their fortifications, as they had to contend with threats from above as well as direct assaults.

The tactical implications of gunpowder artillery extended beyond the immediate effects on siege operations. The psychological impact of artillery was profound—defenders faced the constant threat of bombardment, which could lead to panic and demoralization. The sound of cannon fire, coupled with the devastation it wrought, instilled fear not only in the hearts of soldiers but also in the civilian populations of besieged cities. This psychological warfare became a crucial element in the strategy of commanders who understood that breaking the will of the enemy could be just as important as physical destruction.

As the technology behind gunpowder artillery evolved, so too did the designs and capabilities of siege weapons. By the 16th and 17th centuries, advances in metallurgy and the understanding of ballistics led to the creation of more sophisticated cannons and mortars. These developments not only improved range and accuracy but also facilitated the construction of larger siege engines capable of firing heavier ordnance. The emergence of such artillery pieces heralded the dawn of a new era in military operations, where siege warfare became more about the strategic use of firepower than the traditional methods of attrition.

In conclusion, the birth of modern siege warfare can be directly attributed to the introduction and evolution of gunpowder artillery. Cannons and mortars emerged as game-changers, allowing besieging forces to breach fortifications with unprecedented speed and efficiency. This shift not only altered the tactics employed in siege warfare but also had lasting implications for military strategy, psychology, and the overall conduct of war. As armies adapted to these new realities, the age of gunpowder artillery heralded the beginning of a more destructive and dynamic approach to warfare, laying the groundwork for the conflicts that would follow in the centuries to come.

The Decline of Traditional Weaponry

The advent of gunpowder in the late medieval period marked a pivotal turning point in military history, fundamentally transforming the landscape of warfare. Prior to this development, traditional weaponry such as swords, bows, and various forms of armor dominated combat. The rise of gunpowder weapons introduced a new paradigm that not only affected battlefield tactics but also precipitated the decline of these longstanding tools of war.

Gunpowder was first developed in China, and its introduction to Europe in the late 14th century heralded the beginning of a new era in warfare. Early gunpowder weapons, such as hand cannons and primitive firearms, were relatively crude but offered significant advantages over traditional arms. While bows and crossbows required years of training to master, firearms could be operated with far less skill and training. This democratization of weaponry meant that armies could field larger numbers of armed soldiers more quickly and efficiently, changing the composition and dynamics of military forces.

One of the most significant impacts of gunpowder weaponry was on cavalry and armored knights. The heavily armored knight, once the epitome of chivalric warfare, found his role increasingly threatened by the development of firearms. Early firearms, despite their inaccuracy and slow reload times, proved devastating against the costly plate armor that knights wore. A well-placed shot could penetrate armor, rendering the knight's expensive defensive gear virtually useless. As a result, the traditional cavalry charge, which had been central to medieval battles, began to lose its effectiveness. Armies began to adapt their strategies, focusing on formations that could withstand gunfire and employing infantry armed with firearms instead.

Moreover, the introduction of artillery fundamentally altered the role of fortifications. Castles and city walls, which had been designed to withstand sieges from traditional weaponry like catapults and trebuchets, were ill-equipped to defend against cannon fire. The power of artillery made it possible to breach even the most formidable defenses, leading to the decline of fortified structures as centers of military power. The shift toward mobile warfare, utilizing artillery to dismantle defenses, further diminished the role of traditional defensive tactics.

The psychological impact of gunpowder weaponry cannot be overstated. The fear of being struck by a projectile from a distance transformed the nature of combat. Traditional warriors who prided themselves on hand-to-hand combat found themselves increasingly outmatched by the capabilities of gunpowder arms. This shift not only affected individual soldiers' morale but also the broader cultural perceptions of honor and valor in warfare. The romanticized ideals of the knightly duel gave way to a more mechanized and less personal form of conflict.

In addition to changing battlefield tactics, the mass production of firearms also influenced the social structures surrounding warfare. The rise of gunpowder armies decreased the dependence on the feudal system, where landowners maintained personal armies of knights. Instead, standing armies became the norm, often funded and maintained by centralized states. This shift marked a significant transition in the role of military power within society, indicating a move toward professional militaries rather than feudal levies.

In conclusion, the decline of traditional weaponry such as swords, bows, and armor was a multifaceted process influenced by the rise of gunpowder weapons. The increased lethality, accessibility, and efficiency of firearms and artillery transformed military tactics and societal structures, rendering many traditional forms of combat obsolete. As warfare evolved, so too did the technologies that defined it, leading to a new era where the power of gunpowder shifted the balance of military might and redefined the nature of conflict.

The Spread of Gunpowder Technology Across Cultures

Gunpowder, a mixture of saltpeter, charcoal, and sulfur, revolutionized warfare and military technology from its inception in China during the 9th century. Its development marked a significant shift in the nature of combat and weaponry, leading to profound changes in military strategy, societal structures, and international relations. The diffusion of gunpowder technology from Asia to Europe and beyond during the late medieval period and early modern era is a compelling narrative of innovation, adaptation, and conflict.

Initially discovered by Chinese alchemists seeking an elixir for immortality, gunpowder was initially used for fireworks and signaling before its potential as a military explosive was recognized. By the 10th century, the Chinese had started using gunpowder in warfare, employing it in simple bombs, rockets, and early firearms. The Song Dynasty's military manuals documented the use of gunpowder in various forms, showcasing its effectiveness in battle.

The spread of gunpowder technology began in earnest along the Silk Road, a vast network of trade routes connecting East and West. This exchange facilitated not just the movement of goods but also ideas and innovations. By the 13th century, as the Mongol Empire expanded, it played a crucial role in disseminating gunpowder technology across Asia into the Middle East and eventually into Europe. The Mongols, equipped with early gunpowder weapons, used them to devastating effect during their conquests, leading to increased awareness and interest in these technologies among the cultures they encountered.

In Europe, the arrival of gunpowder coincided with a period of significant military transformation. The introduction of gunpowder weaponry fundamentally altered medieval combat, which had been dominated by knights and cavalry. The use of cannons began to break down the traditional strongholds of feudal lords, as these powerful new weapons could breach castle walls that had stood for centuries. The Battle of Crécy in 1346, where English longbowmen and emerging gunpowder artillery played pivotal roles, highlighted the changing face of warfare.

Gunpowder technology was further accelerated by the interactions between European powers and the Ottoman Empire, which had adopted and advanced gunpowder weaponry in their own military campaigns. The Ottomans effectively utilized cannons during the siege of Constantinople in 1453, demonstrating the strategic advantages of gunpowder in siege warfare. This event caught the attention of European military leaders, prompting them to invest in the development of similar technologies.

As European powers began to explore and colonize other regions, they carried gunpowder technology with them. The Age of Exploration saw Spanish and Portuguese explorers equipped with firearms and cannons, which they used to establish dominance over indigenous populations in the Americas, Africa, and Asia. This not only facilitated European imperial ambitions but also led to the exchange of military technologies across cultures, as indigenous groups adapted and incorporated gunpowder into their own warfare.

In the following centuries, the manufacturing and refinement of gunpowder weapons continued to evolve. The introduction of flintlock mechanisms and the development of more sophisticated artillery further solidified gunpowder's role in warfare. By the 18th century, gunpowder had become a standard component of military arsenals worldwide, impacting conflicts from the Napoleonic Wars to the American Revolution.

The spread of gunpowder technology is a testament to the dynamic nature of cultural exchange and innovation in warfare. It reshaped military strategies, influenced political power dynamics, and had lasting implications for global history. As societies adopted and adapted gunpowder technologies, the implications of its use extended far beyond the battlefield, affecting social structures, economic systems, and international relations across the globe. The legacy of gunpowder remains significant, as it laid the groundwork for the modern era of warfare and the development of subsequent explosive technologies.

Chapter 7

Renaissance and Early Modern Weaponry

The Evolution of Firearms

The Renaissance and early modern period marked a pivotal era in the evolution of firearms, particularly with the development of flintlock mechanisms and muskets. This transformation in weaponry not only revolutionized military tactics but also had profound implications for warfare and society.

The Transition from Matchlocks to Flintlocks

Before the advent of flintlock firearms, the matchlock mechanism dominated the landscape of gunpowder weaponry. Matchlocks utilized a slow-burning wick that was held in a clamp; when the trigger was pulled, the wick ignited the gunpowder. While functional, matchlocks suffered from several drawbacks. They were cumbersome, slow to fire, and susceptible to adverse weather conditions, which could extinguish the wick before discharge.

The introduction of the flintlock mechanism in the early 17th century represented a significant technological leap. The flintlock used a piece of flint, which, when struck against steel, created a spark that ignited the powder in the pan. This innovation allowed for a more reliable firing mechanism, greater speed, and improved safety. Flintlocks quickly became the standard for military firearms, and their design was refined over the decades, leading to increased efficiency and reliability on the battlefield.

Muskets: The Workhorse of Early Modern Warfare

The musket, a type of long gun designed for infantry use, emerged as the primary firearm of the era. Early muskets were smoothbore weapons, meaning they lacked rifling in the barrel, which limited their accuracy and range. However, they were relatively easy to produce and could fire round balls of lead, making them effective in massed infantry formations. The primary role of muskets was to deliver a devastating volley of firepower against enemy troops, especially in the context of linear tactics prevalent during the 17th and 18th centuries.

As the demand for more effective firearms grew, advancements in musket design followed. The introduction of rifled barrels marked a significant improvement in accuracy and range. By the late 18th century, rifled muskets, such as the British Enfield rifle, began to replace smoothbore muskets in military applications. These rifles featured grooves cut into the barrel, allowing the projectile to spin and stabilize in flight, dramatically improving hitting potential at greater distances.

Impact on Military Tactics

The evolution of firearms during this period fundamentally altered military tactics. The effectiveness of muskets led to the development of new formations and strategies. Infantry units began to adopt tactics that maximized the firepower of their muskets, such as linear formations that allowed soldiers to fire in unison. The "musketeer" became a vital component of military forces across Europe, with armies increasingly relying on volley fire to break enemy lines.

Moreover, the evolution of firearms led to significant changes in the role of cavalry. As infantry units became more adept at delivering devastating fire, traditional cavalry charges became riskier and less effective. This shift prompted militaries to rethink their strategies and incorporate new combined-arms tactics that integrated infantry, cavalry, and artillery.

Cultural and Social Implications

The advancements in firearms also had broader implications beyond the battlefield. The increased availability and effectiveness of muskets contributed to changes in social structures, empowering common soldiers and altering the dynamics of power within societies. Firearms became symbols of power, not just for the military but for civilian populations as well, influencing social hierarchies and the nature of governance.

In conclusion, the evolution of firearms, particularly the flintlock and musket, during the Renaissance and early modern period was a critical development in military history. This transformation not only enhanced the effectiveness of armies but also reshaped warfare, tactics, and societal structures, laying the groundwork for future advancements in military technology and strategy. As firearms continued to evolve, they would usher in new challenges and opportunities that would define armed conflict for centuries to come.

The Role of Artillery in Early Modern Warfare

The advent of artillery marked a significant turning point in the landscape of warfare during the early modern period, which spanned roughly from the late 15th century to the early 18th century. This era witnessed the evolution of gunpowder weaponry, including cannons, mortars, and howitzers, fundamentally altering military tactics, fortifications, and the very nature of battle itself.

Initially developed in the late medieval period, artillery gained prominence with the introduction of more sophisticated designs and larger calibers. The use of bronze cannons, for instance, became widespread in the 15th century, followed by the production of iron artillery pieces, which allowed for greater range and destructive power. By the 16th century, the technology had advanced sufficiently to enable cannons to breach the formidable walls of castles and fortified cities that had previously been deemed impregnable.

One of the most notable features of artillery in early modern warfare was its ability to influence the strategic landscape of battles. The presence of cannons forced armies to adapt their formations and tactics. Traditional mass infantry formations, which had been effective in earlier conflicts, became vulnerable to the devastating firepower of artillery. Commanders began to realize that to maintain an advantage on the battlefield, they needed to incorporate artillery into their strategies effectively. This led to the development of new military doctrines, emphasizing the coordination of infantry, cavalry, and artillery units.

Artillery also played a crucial role in sieges, which were a common form of warfare during this period. The ability to destroy defensive walls allowed besieging forces to breach the defenses of fortified cities and strongholds, leading to faster and more decisive victories. Notable examples include the capture of the city of Constantinople in 1453, where the Ottomans employed massive cannons to breach the ancient walls. Such successes showcased the transformative power of artillery and solidified its status as a key component of military operations.

Moreover, the role of artillery extended beyond the battlefield into the realm of logistics and supply chains. The need for specialized training in the operation and maintenance of artillery pieces led to the establishment of artillery corps within armies. These units were tasked with not only firing and positioning cannons but also managing the supply of gunpowder and ammunition, marking a shift towards more organized and professional military structures.

The impact of artillery was also felt in naval warfare during this period. The development of warships equipped with cannons transformed naval battles, allowing for engagements at a distance and changing the tactics of maritime conflict. The introduction of broadside tactics, where ships fired volleys of cannon fire simultaneously, became a hallmark of naval warfare, emphasizing the strategic importance of naval artillery.

Despite the advantages that artillery brought, it was not without challenges. The logistics of transporting heavy artillery pieces and the need for ample supplies of gunpowder created complex operational demands. Additionally, the danger of misfire and the need for skilled gunners added layers of difficulty to its effective use.

In conclusion, artillery emerged as a decisive factor in early modern warfare, reshaping military tactics, siege strategies, and naval engagements. It catalyzed a transition from medieval warfare to a more modern approach, characterized by the integration of various military branches and the development of professional armies. The evolution of artillery not only influenced the outcomes of battles but also left an indelible mark on the strategic and operational paradigms of military history, setting the stage for future advancements in warfare technology.

The Development of Naval Warfare

The evolution of naval warfare is a fascinating study of how maritime conflicts have changed over centuries, influenced by technological advancements, tactical innovations, and the shifting nature of warfare itself. Central to this transformation is the development of ships and cannons, which revolutionized how navies engaged in battle and asserted control over the seas.

Early Naval Combat

Initially, naval combat relied on the use of oared vessels, such as triremes, which were prominent in ancient Mediterranean civilizations. These ships were fast and maneuverable, allowing for tactics like ramming enemy vessels. The Athenian navy, for instance, utilized the trireme effectively during the Persian Wars, demonstrating how superior naval power could enhance a city-state's military strength and influence.

As trade and naval engagements expanded, the need for more durable and versatile vessels became apparent. This led to the development of larger ships, such as the carrack and later the galleon, which could carry more cargo and armaments. These ships were crucial for long-distance trade and exploration, enabling European powers to establish colonies and expand their influence across the globe.

The Advent of Gunpowder

The introduction of gunpowder in the late medieval period marked a pivotal change in naval warfare. Cannons, initially placed on land, were adapted for use on ships, fundamentally altering the nature of naval engagements. By the 15th century, ships began to be equipped with bronze and iron cannons, which provided a range advantage over traditional weaponry like crossbows and ballistae.

The effectiveness of cannons enabled ships to engage enemies from a distance, allowing for a new kind of naval strategy that emphasized broadside attacks. The design of ships also evolved to accommodate heavier artillery. The transition from oared galleys to sailing vessels equipped with cannons led to the rise of the ship of the line—a powerful warship designed for naval battles.

Ships like the English Royal Navy's HMS Victory exemplified this shift, showcasing the combination of speed, maneuverability, and firepower.

Tactical Innovations

As cannons became the dominant weapon of naval warfare, tactics evolved to maximize their effectiveness. The line-of-battle tactic emerged, where ships would form a single line and engage the enemy broadside to broadside. This formation allowed for a concentrated volley of cannon fire, significantly increasing the likelihood of inflicting damage on the opposing fleet.

Naval battles, such as the Battle of Trafalgar in 1805, exemplified this strategic shift. Admiral Nelson's tactics involved breaking the enemy line, allowing his ships to unleash devastating fire upon the enemy while minimizing their own exposure. This battle not only showcased the power of cannon-armed ships but also highlighted the importance of leadership and tactical ingenuity in naval warfare.

The Industrial Revolution and Beyond

The Industrial Revolution brought about further advancements in naval technology. The transition from wood to iron in shipbuilding allowed for greater durability and the construction of ironclad warships, which were impervious to traditional wooden ships and cannon fire. The introduction of steam power also transformed naval warfare, enabling ships to maneuver more effectively regardless of wind conditions.

By the late 19th and early 20th centuries, the development of dreadnoughts—battleships with heavy artillery and steam propulsion—represented the pinnacle of naval warfare technology. Such ships dominated naval engagements during World War I, where battles like Jutland showcased the importance of battleship fleets in asserting national power.

Conclusion

The evolution of naval warfare through the development of ships and cannons illustrates the interplay between technology and military strategy. From the oared vessels of ancient times to the ironclads and dreadnoughts of modern warfare, each advancement has shaped naval tactics and the geopolitical landscape. As navies continue to adapt to new technologies, including unmanned vessels and advanced missile systems, the legacy of these earlier developments remains a critical foundation for understanding the complexities of naval combat today.

The Duel

The early modern era, spanning roughly from the late 15th century to the late 18th century, was a period marked by significant social, political, and cultural transformations in Europe and beyond. One of the most fascinating phenomena of this time was the practice of dueling—a ritualized form of combat that emerged as a means of settling disputes, particularly those related to honor and personal reputation. The cultural significance of dueling cannot be overstated, as it reflected broader societal values, including notions of masculinity, honor, and the evolving nature of warfare.

Dueling became particularly prominent among the nobility and the upper classes, where honor was paramount. In a society where social status and reputation could dictate one's standing and opportunities, the act of challenging an opponent to a duel was often seen as a necessary response to insults, slights, or perceived dishonor. The duel embodied the belief that a man's honor could only be restored through personal combat. Failure to engage in a duel could result in social ostracism, as it was viewed as a sign of cowardice. As such, dueling was not just a personal matter but a public spectacle that reinforced social hierarchies and cultural norms.

The weapons used in dueling varied over time and by region, but they were typically selected for their ability to reflect both the skill of the combatants and the gravity of the encounter. Early duels often employed swords, particularly the rapier—a long, slender blade that allowed for quick thrusts and intricate fencing techniques. The rapier became a symbol of the gentleman duelist, representing both elegance and lethal capability. Its use required training and finesse, underscoring the idea that dueling was not merely a matter of brute force but rather a test of skill, honor, and personal integrity.

As firearms became more prevalent, the nature of dueling evolved. By the 17th and 18th centuries, pistols began to replace swords as the weapon of choice for many duels, particularly in England and France. The introduction of pistols added a new layer of complexity to the practice, as it shifted the focus from physical prowess to marksmanship and nerve. The "dueling pistol" was often a finely crafted weapon, and its presentation was as significant as its functionality. Duelists would often engage in elaborate rituals before the fight, including the choice of weapons, the location of the duel, and even the selection of seconds—trusted friends who would act as witnesses and mediators.

The ritualization of dueling led to the establishment of formal codes of conduct, which sought to regulate the practice and minimize unnecessary bloodshed. These codes outlined the circumstances under which a duel could be fought, the appropriate weapons, and the procedures to be followed. Such regulations reflected the desire for a degree of civility in what was essentially a violent act. However, despite these efforts, dueling remained a dangerous endeavor, with many participants suffering serious injury or death.

The decline of dueling in the 19th century can be attributed to several factors, including the rise of legal systems that provided alternatives for conflict resolution and changing societal attitudes toward violence and honor. Nevertheless, the cultural legacy of dueling persisted, influencing literature, art, and popular perceptions of masculinity and honor. The duel remains a potent symbol of the complexities of human relationships, the weight of social expectations, and the lengths to which individuals would go to defend their reputations.

In conclusion, dueling in the early modern era epitomized a unique intersection of honor, social status, and weaponry. The choice of weapons, the rituals surrounding duels, and the societal implications of this practice offer a rich tapestry through which to explore the values and conflicts of the time. The duel was not merely a violent confrontation but a profound reflection of the cultural dynamics that defined an era.

The Impact of Weaponry on Exploration and Colonization

The era of European exploration and colonization, particularly from the late 15th century to the early 19th century, was profoundly influenced by advancements in weaponry. These innovations not only facilitated the outward expansion of European powers but also significantly altered the dynamics of power in newly encountered regions. The intersection of technological advancement in military hardware and the ambitions of colonial powers reshaped the world's geopolitical landscape.

Technological Superiority

One of the most decisive factors in the success of European explorers and colonizers was their technological superiority in weaponry. The introduction of gunpowder weaponry, including cannons and firearms, provided European forces with a significant advantage over indigenous populations who often relied on traditional weapons such as bows, spears, and axes. The use of cannons aboard ships enabled European navies to dominate the seas, allowing for the establishment of maritime empires. For instance, the Portuguese and Spanish fleets utilized heavy artillery to overpower enemy ships and coastal fortifications during their expeditions.

The effectiveness of firearms, particularly matchlocks and later flintlocks, transformed land engagements. European soldiers, equipped with muskets, could engage enemies from a distance, creating a tactical advantage that often led to overwhelming victories in battles against indigenous forces. The psychological impact of these weapons also played a crucial role; the mere sight of organized, armed European troops could instill fear in local populations, often leading to the swift submission of communities without significant resistance.

The Role of Fortifications

As European powers established colonies, they also constructed fortified settlements and trading posts. The design and implementation of these fortifications were directly influenced by advancements in artillery technology. Strongholds were built to withstand cannon fire and protect against potential uprisings or attacks from indigenous groups. For example, the Spanish established fortified cities such as Cartagena in Colombia and the French built Fort Louisbourg in Canada, which served as critical military and economic hubs within their colonial territories.

These fortifications not only secured European settlements but also served as bases for further exploration and conquest. The protection offered by these strongholds allowed European powers to project their military might across vast distances, facilitating the establishment of control over trade routes and resource-rich areas.

The Impact on Indigenous Populations

The consequences of superior weaponry were catastrophic for many indigenous populations. European colonizers often utilized their military technology to subjugate communities, leading to widespread violence, displacement, and, in many cases, the decimation of local populations through warfare and the spread of diseases to which the indigenous peoples had no immunity. The Aztec and Inca empires, for instance, fell swiftly to Spanish conquistadors, whose advanced weaponry and tactics outmatched the indigenous armies.

Moreover, the introduction of European weaponry altered existing power structures among indigenous groups, as those who acquired European arms often gained an upper hand in inter-tribal conflicts. This dynamic sometimes led to further destabilization of local societies, facilitating European exploitation.

Conclusion

In summary, the advances in weaponry during the age of exploration and colonization fundamentally shaped the interactions between European powers and the rest of the world. The technological superiority provided by firearms and artillery enabled European colonizers to assert dominance over vast territories, often at the expense of indigenous populations and their cultures. This period marked a significant turning point in global history, with weaponry serving as both a tool of expansion and a catalyst for profound social and political changes that would resonate throughout subsequent centuries. The effects of these developments continue to be felt today, as they laid the groundwork for the modern world and its geopolitical complexities.

Chapter 8

Industrial Revolution and the Rise of Modern Warfare

The Impact of the Industrial Revolution on Weapons Manufacturing

The Industrial Revolution, spanning from the late 18th century to the early 19th century, marked a significant turning point not only in manufacturing but also in the realm of military technology and warfare. The shift from manual labor and artisanal production to mechanized manufacturing fundamentally transformed how weapons were produced, leading to significant changes in the scale and nature of warfare. This era saw the introduction of new technologies, techniques, and organizational structures that allowed for the mass production of arms, drastically altering military strategy and the scale of conflicts.

Prior to the Industrial Revolution, weapons manufacturing was predominantly a craft-based activity, characterized by small-scale workshops where skilled artisans hand-forged swords, muskets, and cannons. This limited production capacity meant that armies were often reliant on the availability of skilled labor and could only equip a fraction of their forces with advanced weaponry. The onset of the Industrial Revolution introduced a range of innovations, including the mechanization of production processes, the introduction of assembly lines, and advancements in metallurgy and materials science. These changes enabled the production of weapons on an unprecedented scale.

One of the most significant advancements during this period was the introduction of interchangeable parts in weapon manufacturing. Pioneered by figures such as Eli Whitney, this concept allowed for the mass production of standardized components that could be easily assembled into functional firearms. This not only streamlined the manufacturing process but also facilitated repairs and maintenance, as damaged parts could be replaced quickly and efficiently. The ability to produce large quantities of uniform weapons meant that armies could be equipped more rapidly, dramatically increasing their fighting capacity.

The growth of factories also meant that weapons could be produced in much greater quantities than ever before. The expansion of the iron and steel industries provided the necessary materials for making stronger and more durable weapons. The introduction of steam power and later electricity in manufacturing processes further accelerated production capabilities. By the time of the American Civil War (1861-1865), for instance, weapons such as rifled muskets and repeating firearms were being produced in the millions, allowing armies to engage in conflicts with greater lethality and efficiency.

Moreover, the Industrial Revolution facilitated advancements in artillery technology. The introduction of rifled cannons and breech-loading artillery significantly improved the range and accuracy of field guns. This advancement changed the dynamics of battlefield engagements, allowing armies to strike from a distance and altering traditional tactics that had relied on close formations and charges. The increased firepower also led to higher casualty rates, prompting military strategists to rethink troop deployments and battlefield strategies.

The revolution in weapons manufacturing had profound geopolitical implications as well. Nations that embraced industrialization gained a distinct advantage over those that remained reliant on traditional methods of warfare. The ability to produce advanced weaponry quickly and in large numbers allowed for rapid military mobilization, reshaping the balance of power on the global stage. Countries such as Britain, France, and Germany leveraged their industrial capabilities to expand their empires and influence, often leading to conflicts driven by competition for resources and markets.

In conclusion, the Industrial Revolution represented a watershed moment in the history of weapon manufacturing. Its impact on the scale and nature of warfare was profound, enabling mass production, improving weapon efficiency, and altering military strategies. As nations embraced industrialization, the fundamental dynamics of warfare shifted, leading to larger and more destructive conflicts that would characterize the modern era of warfare. The legacy of these changes continues to resonate today, as the principles of mass production and technological advancement remain central to military logistics and strategy.

The Introduction of Rifled Firearms

The advent of rifled firearms in the early modern period marked a pivotal transition in military technology, fundamentally altering the dynamics of warfare. Prior to the introduction of rifling, smoothbore muskets dominated the battlefield. These weapons, while relatively easy to load and manufacture, suffered from significant limitations in accuracy and effective range. A smoothbore musket could generally be expected to hit a target at a distance of around 50 to 100 yards, with a high degree of variability due to the lack of stability imparted to the projectile during flight.

Rifling technology, which involves the spiral grooves cut into the interior of a gun barrel, revolutionized this landscape. The rifling engages the projectile as it is fired, imparting a spin that stabilizes its flight, much like a thrown football. This spin reduces turbulence and drift, allowing for a straighter trajectory over greater distances. As a result, rifles equipped with rifled barrels could achieve effective ranges of 300 yards or more, significantly improving accuracy and lethality.

The origins of rifled firearms can be traced back to the late 15th century, with the first recorded use of rifled barrels in Europe. Initially, these weapons were not widely adopted, primarily due to the complexity of manufacturing and the slower loading times associated with rifling. However, by the 17th century, the advantages of rifled firearms began to gain recognition, particularly among sharpshooters and specialized military units. The development of the rifle was further propelled by advancements in metallurgy and gunpowder technology, which allowed for the production of stronger, lighter barrels that could withstand the pressures of rifled ammunition.

One of the most significant early examples of rifled firearms was the Pennsylvania rifle, developed in the 18th century by American gunsmiths. This weapon was characterized by its long barrel and precise rifling, making it highly effective for hunting and military skirmishes. The accuracy of the Pennsylvania rifle allowed American colonial forces to engage British troops from a distance, changing the nature of engagements during the American Revolutionary War. Notably, this rifle's effectiveness underscored the importance of marksmanship, leading to the establishment of rifle regiments that trained soldiers in the art of precision shooting.

The advancement of rifling culminated in the mid-19th century with the invention of the Minié ball, a conical bullet that expanded upon firing, allowing for easier loading in rifled barrels while maintaining the projectile's stability in flight. This innovation, coupled with the widespread adoption of rifled muskets during the American Civil War, showcased the devastating impact of rifled firearms on traditional battle tactics. Soldiers armed with rifled muskets could engage enemies at much greater distances, leading to a reevaluation of battlefield formations and strategies.

The impact of rifled firearms extended beyond mere accuracy; they also influenced the psychology of warfare. The ability to engage an enemy from a distance encouraged a shift towards more defensive tactics, as soldiers sought cover and concealment to mitigate the risk of being targeted by accurate rifle fire. This shift was particularly evident in the trenches of World War I, where the lethality of rifled firearms necessitated new approaches to both offense and defense.

In conclusion, the introduction of rifled firearms fundamentally transformed military engagements by enhancing accuracy and range. This technological advancement not only improved the effectiveness of individual soldiers but also reshaped the strategies and tactics employed in warfare. As firearms technology continued to evolve, the principles established by rifling would pave the way for modern weaponry, underscoring the enduring legacy of this critical innovation.

The Machine Gun

The invention of the machine gun marked a pivotal moment in the history of warfare, fundamentally altering battlefield tactics and the dynamics of military engagements. Emerging in the late 19th century, this innovative weapon represented a significant leap from traditional firearms, allowing for sustained, rapid fire that could deliver devastating firepower in a fraction of the time required by manual loading rifles.

Historical Context

The machine gun's roots can be traced back to the late 1800s, with notable developments by inventors such as Hiram Maxim, who created the Maxim Gun in 1884. This weapon utilized the energy generated from the recoil of the fired bullet to automatically load the next round, enabling a single operator to fire hundreds of rounds per minute. Initially met with skepticism, the machine gun would soon prove its worth in various conflicts, including the colonial wars and the First World War.

Tactical Revolution

The introduction of the machine gun led to a dramatic shift in military tactics. Prior to its widespread use, infantry units relied on linear formations, engaging in direct confrontations with enemy lines. However, the rapid-fire capability of machine guns made such formations obsolete; soldiers could no longer advance without facing an overwhelming hail of bullets. This shift forced armies to adopt new strategies, including the use of trenches and cover, which became emblematic of World War I combat.

During World War I, the machine gun became a key component of both offensive and defensive strategies. Its ability to deliver a high volume of fire allowed defending forces to hold their positions against attacking troops, leading to a stalemate on the Western Front. The famous trench warfare characterized by long, drawn-out battles was largely a result of this new firepower, as both sides sought to outmaneuver and outgun each other while remaining protected from machine gun fire.

Impact on Warfare

The psychological impact of the machine gun was equally significant. The sheer volume of fire and the ability to inflict mass casualties changed the nature of soldiering. Troops faced the grim reality of warfare where survival depended not just on strategy but on the ability to withstand the relentless onslaught of machine gun fire. The machine gun also introduced the concept of suppressive fire, where one unit would provide cover for others to maneuver, fundamentally changing the roles of infantry in combat.

As the war progressed, the use of machine guns prompted the development of new tactics, such as the deployment of tanks and armored vehicles designed to withstand enemy fire and support infantry assaults. This led to a more mobile form of warfare, where the integration of machine guns with other technologies began to shape modern military operations.

Conclusion

The machine gun not only revolutionized battlefield tactics but also set the stage for the future of warfare. Its introduction necessitated innovations in military strategy, troop formations, and battlefield technology. The legacy of the machine gun continues to influence military doctrine today, as armies adapt to the ever-evolving landscape of warfare. By enabling unprecedented rates of fire, the machine gun redefined the relationship between soldiers and their weapons, making it one of the most consequential inventions in the history of armaments. As we reflect on its impact, it serves as a reminder of how advancements in weapon technology can shape the course of human conflict, underscoring the need for careful consideration of the ethical implications surrounding the development and use of such powerful tools.

The Role of Railways and Logistics in Modern Warfare

The advent of railways in the 19th century marked a significant turning point in the realm of military logistics and strategy. As nations industrialized, the ability to transport troops, equipment, and supplies quickly and efficiently became paramount. The integration of railways into military planning transformed the scale and nature of warfare, facilitating not just the rapid mobilization of forces but also the sustained logistical support necessary for modern combat operations.

Rapid Troop Mobilization

One of the most profound impacts of railways was the speed at which armies could be assembled and deployed. Prior to the railway age, moving troops over long distances was a labor-intensive and time-consuming process, often taking weeks or months. The introduction of rail transport allowed armies to mobilize quickly in response to threats, enabling them to concentrate forces at critical points on the battlefield with unprecedented speed. For instance, during the American Civil War, both the Union and Confederate armies utilized rail networks to move troops and supplies, which played a crucial role in several key battles. The ability to move entire divisions within hours rather than days or weeks redefined operational strategies.

Efficient Supply Lines

Beyond troop movement, railways played a critical role in establishing efficient supply lines. Effective logistics is essential in sustaining military operations, and railways provided a reliable means of transporting ammunition, food, medical supplies, and equipment to the front lines. For example, during World War I, the extensive use of railway systems allowed for the rapid replenishment of supplies to trench-bound soldiers, which was vital in maintaining morale and combat effectiveness. The ability to move vast quantities of resources quickly meant that armies could engage in prolonged campaigns without the constant threat of supply shortages.

Strategic Infrastructure

Railways also became strategic assets in warfare, often targeted by enemy forces to disrupt supply chains. Recognizing their importance, military planners began to consider railway lines in their strategies, leading to the development of tactics specifically aimed at protecting or destroying rail networks. The destruction of railroads could cripple an enemy's ability to sustain its forces, as seen in various conflicts such as the Russo-Japanese War, where targeted strikes on railway lines significantly hampered the Russian military's operational capabilities.

Innovations in Logistics Management

The reliance on railways necessitated advances in logistics management practices. Military logistics became a specialized field, with the need for accurate forecasting of supply requirements, scheduling of transport, and coordination of multiple moving parts. Rail networks required precise scheduling to ensure that trains carrying troops and materials arrived at the right time and place. This led to the development of sophisticated logistical frameworks that not only improved military efficiency but also had wider implications for national infrastructure and industrial capacity.

The Interplay with Other Modes of Transport

While railways revolutionized military logistics, they also necessitated integration with other forms of transport, such as trucks, ships, and aircraft. The combination of rail transport with road and air logistics created a multi-modal transportation network that enhanced the military's ability to project power globally. For instance, during World War II, the Allies utilized a combination of railways and trucks to move troops and supplies across Europe, demonstrating the necessity of integrating different transport systems for effective military operations.

Conclusion

In summary, the role of railways and logistics in modern warfare cannot be overstated. The capacity for rapid troop mobilization and efficient supply chains transformed military strategy, enabling nations to conduct warfare on a scale previously unimaginable. As logistics became a critical component of military planning, the interplay between transportation technologies and military operations laid the groundwork for contemporary military logistics, which continues to evolve with advancements in technology. The legacy of railways in military logistics remains a testament to the enduring impact of infrastructure on warfare.

The Evolution of Naval and Artillery Technology

The Industrial Revolution, spanning the late 18th to the early 19th centuries, marked a turning point in military history, particularly in the realms of naval and artillery technology. This period was characterized by rapid technological advancements, which fundamentally transformed how wars were fought at sea and on land. The transition from traditional wooden sailing ships to ironclad vessels and the evolution from muzzle-loading cannons to breech-loading artillery pieces set the stage for modern warfare.

Advancements in Naval Technology

The advent of steam power revolutionized naval warfare. Before the Industrial Revolution, naval vessels relied exclusively on wind for propulsion, which limited their maneuverability and speed. The introduction of steam engines enabled ships to travel independently of wind conditions, thus enhancing their operational range and effectiveness. Steam-powered vessels could engage in battles with greater agility, allowing for more complex naval tactics.

The development of ironclad warships during the mid-19th century was another significant milestone. The first notable ironclad, the HMS Warrior, was launched in 1860, featuring iron armor plating that provided unprecedented protection against traditional wooden ships and artillery. Ironclads represented a shift from wooden hulls to metal constructions, leading to the obsolescence of wooden ships as the dominant naval force. The iconic clash between the USS Monitor and the CSS Virginia during the American Civil War in 1862 exemplified the effectiveness of ironclad technology and heralded a new era in naval warfare.

Moreover, the introduction of rifled cannons—artillery pieces with spiral grooves in their barrels—greatly increased range and accuracy. These advancements allowed naval artillery to engage enemy ships from greater distances, making naval skirmishes more lethal and strategic. The combination of steam power, ironclad hulls, and rifled artillery fundamentally altered naval engagements, leading to a new paradigm in maritime conflict.

Transformations in Artillery Technology

Parallel to advancements in naval technology, artillery underwent significant transformations during the Industrial Revolution. The transition from muzzle-loading cannons to breech-loading artillery represented a major innovation. Muzzle-loading cannons required soldiers to load gunpowder and projectiles from the front, a process that was slow and cumbersome, especially under combat conditions. In contrast, breech-loading artillery allowed for quicker loading from the rear, which significantly improved the rate of fire and operational efficiency of artillery units.

The introduction of more powerful explosives, such as smokeless powder, further enhanced artillery performance. Smokeless powder produced less smoke than traditional black powder, improving visibility on the battlefield and allowing artillery units to remain concealed after firing. This innovation provided a tactical advantage, enabling artillery crews to fire and reposition without being easily detected by the enemy.

Additionally, the Industrial Revolution facilitated mass production techniques, allowing for the rapid manufacture of artillery pieces and naval vessels. Factories could produce standardized weapons and munitions in large quantities, ensuring that armies and navies were better equipped and supplied. This shift toward industrial production not only increased the scale of warfare but also led to the development of more sophisticated weaponry.

Conclusion: The Lasting Impact

The advancements in naval and artillery technology during the Industrial Revolution created a profound impact on military strategy and the nature of warfare. The transition to steam-powered ironclads and the introduction of breech-loading artillery revolutionized how battles were fought, emphasizing speed, maneuverability, and the importance of technological superiority. These innovations set the stage for the global conflicts of the 20th century, demonstrating how industrial advancements transformed military capabilities and reshaped the geopolitical landscape. As nations embraced these changes, the consequences of industrial warfare would resonate for generations, influencing tactics, strategies, and the very fabric of military engagement.

Chapter 9

World War I

The Trench Warfare Experience

World War I, often referred to as the Great War, witnessed a dramatic transformation in the nature of warfare, particularly characterized by the emergence of trench warfare. This brutal form of combat necessitated a re-evaluation of weaponry, as soldiers found themselves in static, fortified positions, leading to a unique battlefield experience defined by the use of rifles, bayonets, and grenades.

The Rifle: The Primary Weapon of WWI Infantry

The rifle was the backbone of infantry tactics during World War I. The most prominent model used was the bolt-action rifle, notably the British Lee-Enfield, the German Mauser Gewehr 98, and the French Lebel. These rifles were accurate and efficient, capable of firing multiple rounds per minute, which made them effective for long-range engagements. Soldiers were trained to be proficient marksmen, as the ability to hit targets from a distance was crucial in the vast, open fields and muddy trenches of the Western Front.

However, the static nature of trench warfare led to fierce and deadly confrontations. Soldiers often faced enemy fire while trying to navigate the treacherous terrain of no man's land, the desolate area between opposing trenches. This environment demanded not only accuracy but also rapid-fire capabilities. As a result, infantry tactics evolved to include strategies for massed fire, where soldiers would coordinate their shooting to overwhelm enemy forces.

The Bayonet: A Tool of Close Combat

While rifles dominated the battlefield, the bayonet emerged as a vital tool for close-quarters combat. Attached to the muzzle of a rifle, the bayonet turned the firearm into a stabbing weapon, enabling soldiers to engage in hand-to-hand fighting when charging the enemy trench. The psychological impact of the bayonet charge was significant, as it created a visceral fear in opponents and instilled a sense of bravery in the attacking troops.

The conditions of trench warfare made it essential for soldiers to adapt quickly to sudden, up-close confrontations. The bayonet became a symbol of infantry valor, embodying the brutal reality of combat, where survival often hinged on sheer physicality and aggression. However, the close combat that marked these engagements was fraught with danger, as soldiers were exposed to gunfire and the chaos of battle.

The Grenade: An Innovation in Trench Warfare

As trench warfare evolved, so did the need for weapons capable of breaching enemy defenses without the need for direct engagement. Hand grenades became a crucial addition to the infantry arsenal. Initially derived from earlier designs, such as the stick grenade, the grenade allowed soldiers to launch explosive projectiles into enemy trenches, targeting confined spaces effectively.

The introduction of the "Mills bomb" by the British and the "Stielhandgranate" by the Germans revolutionized close-quarter combat, providing infantrymen with a means to inflict casualties without the need for a direct assault. Soldiers would often use grenades to clear out enemy bunkers or to disrupt enemy formations during a charge. The effectiveness of grenades also led to the development of grenade-throwing techniques and tactics, as soldiers learned to use cover and angles to maximize their lethality.

Conclusion

The experience of trench warfare during World War I fundamentally changed the landscape of battle, with rifles, bayonets, and grenades defining a new era of combat. Each weapon played a distinct role in the strategies employed by soldiers as they faced the grim realities of static warfare and brutal confrontations. The trench emerged as both a defensive stronghold and a deadly battleground, where these weapons dictated the pace and nature of conflict. The horrors of trench warfare, characterized by a reliance on these tools, left an indelible mark on military history, influencing subsequent warfare strategies and weapon development in the years to come.

The Introduction of Chemical Warfare

World War I marked a pivotal shift in the nature of warfare, introducing advanced technologies that fundamentally altered the battlefield landscape. Among these innovations was the emergence of chemical warfare, a gruesome tactic that represented the darker capabilities of modern science and industry. Chemical weapons, designed to inflict harm, panic, and confusion, became a hallmark of the Great War, showcasing the devastating impact of mass destruction weapons on both military personnel and civilian populations.

Chemical warfare had its roots in earlier conflicts, but it was during WWI that it was systematically deployed on a large scale. The first significant use of chemical agents occurred at the Second Battle of Ypres in April 1915, when German forces released chlorine gas against Allied troops. This marked the first time that a major military force utilized chemical weapons in combat, creating a terrifying precedent. The initial deployment caused immediate and horrific effects, leading to choking, disorientation, and often death for those who inhaled it. The psychological impact was profound; soldiers faced a new kind of enemy—one that could strike without warning and from a distance.

Following chlorine gas, a variety of other chemical agents were developed and employed throughout the war. Phosgene and tear gas were other widely used substances. Phosgene, in particular, proved to be more lethal than chlorine gas, causing delayed reactions that made it particularly insidious. By the end of the war, the deployment of chemical weapons was not limited to one side; both the Allies and the Central Powers engaged in chemical warfare, with each seeking to outdo the other in the development of more effective agents.

The use of chemical weapons lead to a myriad of tactical changes on the battlefield. Troops were forced to adapt to the new threat by donning gas masks and developing protective measures, significantly altering training and combat strategies. However, the protective gear was not always effective. The masks were often uncomfortable and could not fully prevent exposure, particularly in windy conditions. Additionally, the gas attacks frequently drifted unpredictably, endangering both attackers and defenders.

The impact of chemical warfare extended beyond the battlefield. The indiscriminate nature of chemical agents often affected civilian populations, leading to widespread condemnation and ethical debates about the nature of warfare. The horrors associated with chemical attacks contributed to a growing awareness of the need for regulations governing their use. By the end of the war, the international community recognized the need for frameworks to ban such weapons, culminating in the 1925 Geneva Protocol, which prohibited the use of chemical and biological weapons in warfare. However, the effectiveness of the protocol was limited, as it did not address the development or stockpiling of these weapons.

The legacy of chemical warfare in WWI is one of profound horror and moral ambiguity. It illustrated the extent to which technological advancements could be weaponized, leading to unprecedented levels of suffering. While chemical weapons were initially seen as a strategic advantage, their use raised significant ethical questions about humanity's capacity for destruction. The experience of WWI left a lasting impression on military strategy and international law, shaping future discussions about the moral implications of warfare and the need for comprehensive disarmament efforts in the years to come. Thus, chemical warfare not only changed the dynamics of battle but also ignited a broader conversation about the responsibility of nations to regulate the means of war in an increasingly perilous world.

The Tank

The development of the tank during World War I marked a pivotal transformation in land warfare, fundamentally altering military strategies and the nature of combat. As the war progressed, traditional tactics, which relied heavily on infantry and cavalry, became increasingly ineffective against the entrenched positions of enemy forces. The stalemate of trench warfare, characterized by a gridlock of defenses that led to massive casualties and minimal territorial gains, necessitated a new approach to breaking through the front lines.

The origins of the tank can be traced back to the early 20th century, where military leaders began to realize the limitations of existing weaponry against fortified positions. The British Army, in particular, took the lead in conceptualizing a vehicle that could traverse rough terrain, withstand enemy fire, and provide mobile firepower. The initial prototypes, known as "land ships," were designed to crush barbed wire and cross trenches, offering a solution to the logistical challenges of trench warfare.

The first tanks, such as the British Mark I, debuted on the battlefield in September 1916 during the Battle of the Somme. These early models were far from perfect, often suffering from mechanical failures, slow speeds, and limited firepower. However, they demonstrated the potential of armored warfare, showcasing how a vehicle could shield soldiers while allowing for offensive maneuvers. The introduction of tracks allowed tanks to move across diverse terrains, including muddy fields and shell-riddled landscapes, which were previously impassable for traditional vehicles.

As tank technology evolved, so did their tactical application. By the end of World War I, tanks had begun to fulfill several vital roles on the battlefield. They provided direct support to infantry, broke through enemy lines, and targeted artillery positions, significantly enhancing the offensive capabilities of military forces. The psychological impact of tanks also cannot be understated; their imposing presence on the battlefield demoralized enemy troops and disrupted established defensive strategies.

The interwar period saw further advancements in tank design, with an emphasis on speed, firepower, and mobility. The development of more powerful engines and better armaments transformed tanks from slow-moving behemoths into fast, versatile units. Nations began to invest heavily in armored divisions, recognizing the tank's potential as a decisive factor in future conflicts.

World War II would witness the full realization of the tank's capabilities. The Blitzkrieg tactics employed by Germany during the early years of the war exemplified the effective use of tanks in combined arms operations. Fast-moving tank units, supported by infantry and air power, were able to encircle and overwhelm enemy forces, achieving rapid victories that reshaped the European battlefield. The introduction of the Panzer divisions demonstrated the lethal efficiency of tanks when used in coordinated assaults, leading to the fall of several nations in quick succession.

Moreover, the contrasting designs of tanks during World War II reflected differing military philosophies. The Soviet T-34, with its sloped armor and powerful 76mm gun, symbolized an approach that prioritized mass production and ease of repair, while the German Tiger tank represented a focus on heavy armor and firepower, albeit at the cost of mobility and logistical complexity.

In conclusion, the tank's development during World War I and its subsequent evolution into a central element of modern warfare underscored the necessity for innovation in military strategy. The ability of tanks to break the stalemate of trench warfare not only changed the course of battles but also established them as essential components of ground forces in the decades that followed. The lessons learned from the introduction of tanks continue to inform contemporary military doctrine, as armored vehicles remain a critical aspect of land warfare strategies around the globe.

Aerial Combat

The advent of World War I marked a pivotal moment in military history, fundamentally transforming the nature of warfare through the introduction of aerial combat. Although the airplane was a relatively new invention at the outset of the war, its potential as a military asset quickly became apparent. The role of aircraft evolved rapidly, transitioning from simple reconnaissance tools to critical components of combat operations.

Initially, the primary function of aircraft in World War I was reconnaissance. As the war began in 1914, commanders recognized the need for aerial observation to gather intelligence on enemy troop movements, supply lines, and fortifications. Early aircraft, often unarmed and equipped with cameras, soared above the battlefields, providing crucial information that ground forces could leverage. Pilots would fly high above enemy lines, capturing images that would inform strategic decisions and operations. This reconnaissance capability offered commanders a significant advantage, allowing for more informed tactical planning.

However, as the war progressed, the necessity for protection and domination of the skies became equally vital. This led to the emergence of armed aerial combat, as pilots began equipping their aircraft with machine guns. The first recorded instance of aerial combat occurred in 1914, when pilots engaged in dogfights, maneuvering their planes to gain an advantage over adversaries. The introduction of synchronizer gear allowed pilots to fire their weapons through the propeller arc without damaging the blades, significantly increasing the effectiveness of aircraft in combat. This innovation marked a turning point, as aerial engagements became a staple of military strategy.

The rise of fighter aces—pilots who achieved multiple aerial victories—captured public imagination and became symbols of national pride. Notable figures like the Red Baron, Manfred von Richthofen, emerged, demonstrating the human element of aerial warfare. Their exploits were widely reported in newspapers, contributing to a romanticized view of aerial combat that overshadowed the grim realities of war. The development of specialized fighter aircraft, such as the Sopwith Camel and the Fokker Dr.I, showcased advancements in speed, maneuverability, and firepower, leading to more intense and strategic dogfights.

Bombing operations also evolved during World War I, as militaries recognized the potential of aircraft to deliver payloads directly to enemy positions. Early bombers, such as the Handley Page Type O, conducted strategic bombing raids targeting supply depots, railway lines, and even civilian infrastructure. These missions aimed to disrupt enemy logistics and morale, illustrating the duality of aerial warfare that encompassed both tactical and psychological dimensions. The scale of bombing operations would expand significantly in subsequent conflicts, but World War I laid the groundwork for the strategic use of bombers in warfare.

As World War I drew to a close in 1918, the role of aircraft had irrevocably changed military operations. Aerial combat had transitioned from a novel concept to an essential aspect of warfare, influencing tactics, strategy, and the overall conduct of military campaigns. The lessons learned during this period would shape future conflicts, with air power becoming a decisive factor in World War II and beyond.

In conclusion, the dawn of military aviation during World War I heralded the beginning of aerial combat as a critical component of modern warfare. From reconnaissance to dogfights and bombing raids, the evolution of aircraft in this era not only transformed military tactics but also established the foundation for the air power strategies that would dominate the 20th century and beyond. The legacy of World War I aviation continues to resonate today, as air power remains a cornerstone of military operations worldwide.

Naval Warfare in WWI

World War I marked a significant turning point in naval warfare, characterized by the fierce competition between battleships and submarines. The conflict highlighted the strategic importance of naval power and introduced innovative technologies that would shape future maritime combat.

At the onset of the war in 1914, battleships were the dominant force of naval fleets. These imposing vessels, heavily armored and equipped with large-caliber guns, symbolized national strength and were considered the backbone of naval strategy. The British Royal Navy and the Imperial German Navy engaged in a naval arms race, leading to the construction of vast fleets that included dreadnoughts—battleships equipped with uniform heavy artillery and steam turbines, allowing for greater speed and firepower.

The Battle of Jutland in 1916 epitomized the clash of battleships. It was the largest naval battle of the war, involving over 250 ships and more than 100,000 men. The British Grand Fleet, commanded by Admiral Sir John Jellicoe, sought to maintain naval superiority against the German High Seas Fleet, commanded by Vice-Admiral Reinhard Scheer. The battle resulted in significant losses for both sides, but the British fleet's ability to absorb the damage and maintain control of the North Sea proved crucial. Despite the tactical draw of Jutland, British naval dominance persisted, primarily due to their superior resources and infrastructure.

However, the introduction of submarines—specifically, German U-boats—revolutionized naval combat. Initially underestimated, these stealthy vessels posed a significant threat to conventional naval powers. The U-boat employed a strategy known as unrestricted submarine warfare, targeting not only military vessels but also merchant ships carrying supplies to the Allies. This tactic aimed to cut off vital supply lines and starve Britain into submission.

The sinking of the RMS Lusitania in 1915, a British ocean liner with American passengers, highlighted the perilous nature of submarine warfare and intensified anti-German sentiment in the United States. The incident prompted a reevaluation of naval strategy among Allied powers, leading to the implementation of convoy systems to protect merchant ships from submarine attacks. This strategy involved grouping cargo ships together, escorted by naval warships, to provide mutual protection against U-boats.

As warfare progressed, submarines became more advanced, with improved torpedo technology and greater operational ranges. The Allies responded with countermeasures, including depth charges and the development of sonar (ASDIC) technology to detect underwater threats. The naval arms race extended beyond battleships and submarines to include innovations such as mines and anti-submarine warfare tactics.

The impact of submarines on naval warfare during WWI extended beyond tactical engagements; it also influenced broader war strategies. The German reliance on U-boats aimed to cripple the British economy and disrupt the flow of supplies to the front lines. Ultimately, the effectiveness of this strategy waned as Allied countermeasures improved and the United States entered the war, providing fresh naval resources and manpower.

In summary, naval warfare during World War I was defined by the intense rivalry between battleships and submarines. While battleships represented traditional naval power, the emergence of U-boats introduced a new dimension of stealth and asymmetric warfare. The conflict laid the groundwork for future naval engagements, illustrating the need for adaptability in military strategies and technologies. As the war concluded, it was clear that the lessons learned from this period would significantly shape naval doctrine in the years to come, foreshadowing the evolving nature of warfare in the 20th century and beyond.

Chapter 10

Interwar Period

The Rise of Mechanized Warfare

The interwar period, spanning from the end of World War I in 1918 to the beginning of World War II in 1939, was a time of significant military innovation and transformation, particularly in the realm of mechanized warfare. The advancements in technology and the lessons learned from World War I greatly influenced the development and deployment of tanks and armored vehicles, revolutionizing battlefield tactics and strategies.

After the horrors of trench warfare in World War I, military leaders recognized the need for more mobile and effective means of combat. The static nature of trench warfare had rendered traditional cavalry and infantry tactics obsolete against fortified positions. In response, the concept of mechanization began to take root, leading to the creation of new armored vehicles that could traverse the battlefield more effectively than their predecessors.

One of the most significant developments during this period was the evolution of the tank. Initially introduced as a solution to break the deadlock of trench warfare, tanks underwent significant improvements based on practical experiences gained during the war. Early models, such as the British Mark I, were bulky and slow, but innovations in design led to the creation of more streamlined, faster, and better-armed vehicles. Countries like Britain, France, and the United States invested heavily in tank design, focusing on enhancing armor protection, increasing firepower, and improving mobility.

The interwar years also saw the emergence of armored doctrines that emphasized the importance of mobility and speed in warfare. Influential military theorists, such as the German General Heinz Guderian, advocated for the use of tanks as part of coordinated mechanized formations that integrated infantry, artillery, and air support. Guderian's ideas culminated in the concept of "Blitzkrieg," or lightning warfare, which emphasized rapid, surprise attacks that would overwhelm enemy defenses before they could react effectively.

The rise of mechanized warfare was not limited to tanks alone; it also included the development of armored vehicles that supported infantry and provided reconnaissance capabilities. Armored personnel carriers and half-tracks became essential components of military strategy, enabling the rapid transport of troops while offering protection from enemy fire. These innovations allowed for greater operational flexibility and the ability to conduct combined arms operations, where various military branches worked in concert.

Countries across the globe recognized the importance of mechanized forces, leading to significant investments in tank production and research. The United States developed the M2 and M3 light tanks, while the Soviet Union focused on producing the T-26, which became one of the most widely used tanks of the era. In contrast, Germany's Panzer divisions became synonymous with the use of armored vehicles in warfare, demonstrating the effectiveness of mechanized units during the invasion of Poland in 1939 and subsequent campaigns.

The interwar period also witnessed the establishment of military exercises that tested the effectiveness of mechanized warfare. Nations conducted large-scale maneuvers to refine tactics and develop strategic doctrines that would ultimately be employed in World War II. These exercises laid the groundwork for the rapid and effective use of armored formations in the early years of the conflict, as nations adapted their strategies to leverage the advantages of mechanization.

In conclusion, the rise of mechanized warfare during the interwar period fundamentally altered the landscape of military conflict. Innovations in tank and armored vehicle design, combined with new tactical doctrines, set the stage for the rapid and mobile warfare that characterized World War II. As nations prepared for the next global conflict, the lessons learned from the past and the advancements made in mechanization would play a pivotal role in shaping the strategies and outcomes of battles on land.

The Evolution of Aircraft

The evolution of aircraft during the 20th century marked a transformative period in military strategy, significantly altering the dynamics of warfare. From the rudimentary biplanes of World War I to the sophisticated jet fighters and bombers of modern conflicts, advancements in aviation technology reshaped how wars were fought and how nations prepared for conflict.

Early Developments

The inception of military aviation can be traced back to World War I, when the first powered aircraft were used primarily for reconnaissance. These early planes offered a strategic advantage by enabling commanders to gain valuable intelligence about enemy troop movements and positions. The introduction of the fighter aircraft, such as the Sopwith Camel and the Fokker Dr.I, marked a significant development in aerial combat. Fighter planes were equipped with machine guns synchronized to fire through the propeller arc, allowing for dogfights that became iconic in the war. This evolution of the aircraft not only changed how battles were fought but also emphasized the importance of air superiority.

The Interwar Period and Technological Advancements
Following World War I, the interwar period saw significant advancements in aircraft design and technology. The introduction of metal structures, more powerful engines, and advancements in aerodynamics allowed for faster, more maneuverable planes. During this time, nations began to recognize the potential of strategic bombing, leading to the development of bombers like the Boeing B-17 Flying Fortress and the Consolidated B-24 Liberator. These heavy bombers could carry substantial payloads over long distances, allowing them to strike at enemy infrastructure and supply lines, thereby crippling the war effort without engaging in ground combat.

World War II: The Golden Age of Military Aviation
World War II marked the zenith of military aviation evolution, with the introduction of advanced fighter planes and bombers that would dominate the skies. The P-51 Mustang, with its long range and powerful engine, exemplified the fighter aircraft's role in achieving air superiority. Simultaneously, the B-29 Superfortress represented the pinnacle of bomber design, capable of carrying out strategic bombing campaigns deep into enemy territory, including the devastating bombings of Hiroshima and Nagasaki.

The war also highlighted the importance of coordination between different types of aircraft. Fighter escorts protected bombers from enemy fighters, while reconnaissance planes such as the P-38 Lightning gathered intelligence crucial for planning operations. The integration of these roles underscored a shift in military strategy, where air power became an essential component of overall warfare, influencing ground and naval operations.

The Cold War: Jet Age and Technological Innovation
As the Cold War emerged, aircraft technology continued to evolve rapidly. The introduction of jet engines revolutionized aerial combat, leading to faster and more agile fighter jets like the F-86 Sabre and the MiG-15. The development of radar and missile technology further transformed air warfare, allowing for beyond-visual-range engagements and altering tactics regarding air defense and attack strategies.

Reconnaissance aircraft, such as the U-2 and later the SR-71 Blackbird, became vital for intelligence gathering, enabling nations to monitor enemy movements and capabilities from high altitudes. This emphasis on reconnaissance underlined the growing importance of information in military strategy, as well as the need for precision in targeting.

Modern Warfare: Unmanned Systems and New Paradigms

In recent decades, the evolution of aircraft has taken a dramatic turn with the advent of unmanned aerial vehicles (UAVs). Drones like the MQ-1 Predator and the MQ-9 Reaper have shifted the paradigm of air combat and reconnaissance, allowing for precision strikes and intelligence gathering without risking pilot lives. This development has further influenced military strategies, emphasizing the need for rapid response and minimal footprint in conflict zones.

In conclusion, the evolution of aircraft—from the biplanes of World War I to the advanced UAVs of today—has profoundly influenced military strategies throughout the 20th and 21st centuries. As technology continues to advance, the role of aircraft in warfare will likely evolve further, reflecting the changing nature of conflicts and the ongoing quest for air superiority and operational effectiveness.

The Development of Naval Power

The evolution of naval power during the late 19th and early 20th centuries was marked by significant advancements in ship design, particularly with the introduction of battleships and aircraft carriers. These vessels not only transformed naval warfare but also reflected the strategic imperatives of the time, as nations recognized the necessity of maintaining a dominant maritime presence.

The Rise of Battleships

Battleships emerged as the preeminent naval vessels following the Industrial Revolution, which brought about technological innovations such as steam power and ironclad hulls. The transition from wooden ships to iron-hulled vessels marked a turning point in naval warfare. The launch of HMS Dreadnought by the British Royal Navy in 1906 epitomized this change; it was the first battleship to feature an all-big-gun armament and steam turbine propulsion, rendering previous designs obsolete. The Dreadnought's speed, heavy armor, and powerful artillery allowed it to dominate engagements, leading to a naval arms race among the great powers of the time.

Battleships became symbols of national pride and military might, serving as floating fortresses equipped with a combination of large-caliber guns, torpedoes, and advanced armor. Their design emphasized firepower and protection, leading to the development of increasingly sophisticated gunnery and targeting systems. The naval strategies of World War I were deeply influenced by the capabilities of these vessels, as nations sought to control sea lanes and project power across the globe.

The Advent of Aircraft Carriers

The introduction of aircraft carriers in the 1920s and 1930s marked a revolutionary shift in naval strategy. Initially viewed as auxiliary vessels, carriers quickly proved their worth as primary instruments of naval power. Unlike battleships, which relied on direct engagement with enemy fleets, aircraft carriers enabled naval forces to project air power over vast distances, altering the nature of naval warfare.

The pivotal moment for aircraft carriers came during World War II, particularly at the Battle of Midway in 1942. In this battle, U.S. Navy carriers successfully launched air strikes that devastated the Japanese fleet, demonstrating that air superiority could decisively influence naval engagements. The ability of carriers to deploy fighter planes and bombers allowed for strategic flexibility, enabling the destruction of enemy ships before they could engage in close combat.

Strategic Implications

The development of both battleships and aircraft carriers necessitated changes in naval strategy. The principle of "control of the seas" became paramount, as nations sought to secure maritime routes vital for trade and military operations. The interplay between battleships and aircraft carriers led to the emergence of combined arms tactics at sea, where naval power was not solely defined by the presence of heavy guns but also by the ability to conduct air operations.

The strategic importance of aircraft carriers grew during the Cold War, as they became central to power projection and deterrence strategies. Nations like the United States and the Soviet Union invested heavily in carrier strike groups, which combined the capabilities of aircraft carriers with destroyers and submarines to create formidable naval forces capable of operating globally.

Conclusion

In summary, the development of naval power through the evolution of battleships and aircraft carriers significantly reshaped naval warfare and strategy. While battleships served as the dominant force for much of the early 20th century, the rise of aircraft carriers introduced a new paradigm, emphasizing the importance of air power in maritime conflicts. As navies adapted to these technological advancements, the balance of power at sea continued to shift, highlighting the ongoing evolution of naval strategy in response to emerging threats and capabilities.

The Role of Small Arms in Modernizing Armies

The evolution of small arms has played a pivotal role in modernizing armies across the globe, shaping not only military tactics but also the very structure and effectiveness of armed forces. Small arms, typically defined as individual firearms designed for use by a single soldier, include rifles, pistols, submachine guns, and light machine guns. Their development and standardization have parallelled significant shifts in warfare, particularly in the 20th and 21st centuries.

Historical Context

The 20th century marked a transformative period in the development of small arms, beginning with the widespread adoption of bolt-action rifles during World War I. These weapons, such as the British Lee-Enfield and the German Mauser, were complemented by the introduction of semi-automatic rifles like the M1 Garand during World War II, which provided soldiers with faster rates of fire and increased accuracy. The integration of small arms into military strategy changed the dynamics of infantry combat, allowing for more versatile and mobile units capable of engaging enemies at various ranges.

Standardization and Interoperability

As armies recognized the advantages of modern small arms, standardization became a crucial focus. Countries began to develop and adopt specific calibers, such as the NATO-standard 5.56x45mm and the Soviet 7.62x39mm, to ensure interoperability among allied forces. This standardization allowed for the easier logistics of ammunition supply and maintenance, as well as the capability for joint operations among coalition forces. The benefits of standardization extend beyond logistics; they also enhance operational effectiveness, as troops can share ammunition and weapon systems without the complications of diverse calibers.

Technological Advancements

The late 20th and early 21st centuries have witnessed remarkable technological advancements in small arms. The introduction of polymer materials has made firearms lighter and more durable, while advancements in optics have improved accuracy and target acquisition. The development of bullpup designs, which place the action behind the trigger, has allowed for shorter and more maneuverable weapons without sacrificing barrel length. These innovations have led to the creation of versatile small arms that can be adapted for various combat scenarios, from urban warfare to open-field engagements.

Moreover, the rise of modular weapon systems has further revolutionized the role of small arms in modern armies. Soldiers can now modify their weapons with attachments such as grenade launchers, suppressors, and advanced sighting systems, allowing for customization to meet specific mission requirements. This flexibility ensures that infantry units are better equipped to handle the diverse challenges presented in modern combat environments.

Implications for Military Doctrine

The continued development and standardization of small arms have profound implications for military doctrine. Modern armies increasingly emphasize combined arms tactics, integrating infantry with armored, artillery, and air support. The effectiveness of small arms in these operations is crucial; they serve as the backbone of infantry units, allowing them to operate effectively in coordination with heavier firepower. Additionally, the emphasis on light infantry and special operations forces has underscored the importance of small arms that are lightweight, reliable, and capable of delivering precise firepower.

Conclusion

In conclusion, the role of small arms in modernizing armies cannot be overstated. From their historical evolution to the technological advancements that continue to redefine their capabilities, small arms have become central to military effectiveness. Standardization and interoperability have enhanced logistical efficiency and operational cohesion among allied forces, while the development of modular systems has allowed for tailored solutions to complex combat scenarios. As warfare continues to evolve, the ongoing innovation in small arms will remain a critical factor in shaping the future of military capabilities and strategies. The integration of these weapons into modern military doctrine highlights the enduring significance of infantry in contemporary warfare, ensuring that small arms will continue to play a vital role in the effectiveness of armed forces worldwide.

The Role of Intelligence and Espionage

Intelligence and espionage have played pivotal roles in military strategy throughout history. As societies evolved and conflicts became more complex, the need for accurate and timely information on enemy movements, capabilities, and intentions grew increasingly crucial. The development of intelligence-gathering and spycraft emerged as essential methodologies for ensuring military success and maintaining national security.

Historical Context

The origins of military intelligence can be traced back to ancient civilizations, such as those of Egypt, Greece, and Rome. Early military leaders recognized the importance of understanding their adversaries to devise effective strategies. For instance, during the Peloponnesian War, the Athenian general Alcibiades employed spies to gather information about the Spartans, enabling him to orchestrate more effective campaigns. Similarly, Roman generals often relied on scouts and informants to keep tabs on enemy movements, which allowed them to outmaneuver opponents on the battlefield.

The Evolution of Espionage Techniques

As warfare evolved, so did the techniques of espionage. The Middle Ages saw the establishment of formal systems of intelligence-gathering, especially in the context of feudal conflicts. Knights and lords employed spies to gather information about rival factions, enhancing their strategic decision-making. The use of coded messages and secret communications became prevalent, with emissaries often tasked to convey sensitive information discreetly.

The Renaissance brought about advancements in technology and communication, further transforming espionage. The invention of the printing press allowed for the dissemination of propaganda and misinformation, while developments in cryptography enabled the secure transmission of intelligence. Notably, during the Reformation, intelligence networks emerged as religious conflicts intensified across Europe, leading to the establishment of spy networks by various monarchs.

The Rise of Modern Intelligence Services

The 19th century marked a significant turning point in the evolution of military intelligence. The Napoleonic Wars highlighted the necessity of systematic intelligence-gathering. Napoleon Bonaparte utilized a network of spies that provided him with strategic insights, allowing him to execute military campaigns with remarkable efficiency. In response, other nations began to formalize their intelligence operations, leading to the creation of dedicated intelligence agencies.

The advent of the 20th century further advanced the sophistication of espionage. The world wars prompted countries to invest heavily in intelligence capabilities. The British Secret Intelligence Service (SIS), for instance, played a crucial role during World War I and II, employing espionage and counterintelligence to protect national interests. The use of coded messages, radio transmissions, and aerial reconnaissance became integral to military strategy, with intelligence significantly influencing the outcomes of key battles.

Intelligence in the Cold War Era

The Cold War ushered in an unprecedented arms race and geopolitical tension, amplifying the importance of intelligence and espionage. Both the United States and the Soviet Union engaged in extensive covert operations to gather information on each other's military capabilities and intentions. The establishment of the Central Intelligence Agency (CIA) and the KGB exemplified the centralization of intelligence efforts, which included not only military espionage but also political and economic intelligence.

Contemporary Implications

In today's global landscape, intelligence and espionage remain vital components of military strategy. The advent of technology has revolutionized intelligence-gathering techniques, with satellite imagery, cyber capabilities, and data analytics playing critical roles. Modern military operations rely heavily on real-time intelligence to inform decision-making, optimize resource allocation, and mitigate risks.

Moreover, the rise of non-state actors and asymmetric warfare has further complicated the intelligence landscape. Terrorist organizations often employ unconventional methods to gather information, necessitating adaptive intelligence strategies. The interplay between technology, espionage, and military strategy continues to evolve, underscoring the enduring significance of intelligence in shaping the outcomes of conflicts.

In conclusion, the role of intelligence and espionage in military strategy has grown increasingly complex and critical throughout history. From ancient scouts to modern intelligence agencies, the effectiveness of military operations hinges on the ability to gather, analyze, and act upon information about adversaries. As warfare continues to evolve, so will the methodologies and technologies that underpin intelligence-gathering, ensuring its place as a cornerstone of military success.

Chapter 11

World War II

Infantry Weapons of World War II

World War II marked a significant evolution in infantry weaponry, as armies across the globe adapted their tactics and technologies to meet the challenges of a total war. The conflict saw the widespread use of rifles, machine guns, and grenades, each playing a critical role in shaping the battlefield dynamics across various theaters of war.

Rifles: The Backbone of Infantry

Rifles were the primary individual weapons used by soldiers during World War II, serving as the backbone of infantry forces. One of the most iconic examples was the American M1 Garand, which was the first semi-automatic rifle to be widely issued to troops. Its ability to fire eight rounds without reloading gave American soldiers a significant advantage in firepower compared to the bolt-action rifles used by many other nations. Similarly, the Soviet Mosin-Nagant and the British Lee-Enfield were standard-issue rifles that provided reliable accuracy and lethality.

Rifles were not only crucial for engaging enemy forces but also served as a symbol of individual soldier capability. Soldiers were trained extensively in marksmanship, as hitting a target at range was essential for survival on the front lines. In urban combat, such as the Battle of Stalingrad or the ruins of Berlin, rifles allowed infantry to engage effectively in close-quarters combat, making them versatile tools of war.

Machine Guns: Firepower and Suppression

Machine guns transformed infantry tactics by providing a means of sustained firepower that could suppress enemy movements and support infantry advances. The German MG42, known for its high rate of fire and effectiveness, became a feared weapon on the battlefield. It was often used to create interlocking fields of fire, making it difficult for enemy troops to advance without taking casualties.

The American Browning M1919 and the Soviet DP-28 also played vital roles in infantry units, providing vital support during attacks and defensive positions. These machine guns were often mounted on vehicles or tripods, allowing them to deliver devastating firepower while maintaining mobility.

In combination with rifles, machine guns changed the nature of infantry engagements. Rather than relying solely on individual marksmanship, units began to coordinate fire, using machine guns to pin down enemy troops while riflemen maneuvered for advantageous positions. This shift in tactics reflected the evolving nature of warfare, where massed firepower became essential for success.

Grenades: Close-Quarters Combat Solutions

Grenades emerged as indispensable tools for infantrymen during World War II, especially in urban and jungle warfare where engagements often occurred at close range. The fragmentation grenade became a standard issue for soldiers, providing an effective means to clear enemy positions or trenches. The American Mk 2 grenade and the German Stielhandgranate (stick grenade) were widely used, each designed to inflict maximum damage in confined spaces.

Grenades allowed soldiers to engage enemies who were hidden or entrenched without exposing themselves to direct fire. This capability was particularly important during assaults on fortified positions, where throwing grenades could neutralize threats before troops moved in. Moreover, grenade tactics evolved, with soldiers often trained to throw them in combination with suppressive fire from rifles and machine guns, creating a lethal synergy on the battlefield.

Conclusion

The use of rifles, machine guns, and grenades during World War II showcased the evolution of infantry weapons and their profound impact on modern warfare. Each weapon type contributed to the overall effectiveness of infantry units, allowing them to adapt to the challenges of a global conflict. The lessons learned in this period would continue to influence military strategy and infantry tactics long after the war concluded, underscoring the critical role that effective infantry weapons play in determining the outcomes of battles.

Armored Warfare

The advent of World War II marked a significant shift in military strategy and technology, with armored warfare emerging as a dominant force on the battlefield. Central to this evolution was the tank, a mechanized vehicle designed for frontline engagement, capable of traversing difficult terrain and delivering both firepower and protection to its crew. The tank's design and deployment would profoundly shape land battles, influencing the strategies of both the Axis and Allied powers throughout the war.

The origins of tank warfare can be traced back to World War I, where tanks were first introduced as a means to break the stalemate of trench warfare. However, it was during World War II that tanks were fully integrated into military tactics, evolving into powerful instruments of warfare.

The German Blitzkrieg strategy exemplified this evolution. It emphasized rapid, coordinated attacks using tanks, infantry, and air support to overwhelm enemy defenses. This approach, characterized by speed and surprise, enabled Germany to achieve early victories in Poland and France, demonstrating the overwhelming effectiveness of armored units in mobile warfare.

The design of tanks during this period saw significant advancements. Early in the war, tanks like the German Panzer III and IV, as well as the British Matilda and Crusader, showcased various innovations in armor, firepower, and mobility. The introduction of sloped armor improved ballistic resistance, while more powerful cannons allowed tanks to engage enemy fortifications and other armored vehicles effectively. The Soviet T-34, introduced in 1940, became a game-changer on the Eastern Front. Its combination of thick armor, a powerful 76.2mm gun, and excellent mobility made it one of the most effective tanks of the war, allowing the Red Army to counter the initial German advances and ultimately push them back.

As the war progressed, the scale and intensity of tank battles escalated. The Battle of El Alamein in North Africa and the Battle of Kursk in the Soviet Union became pivotal moments in the history of armored warfare. At El Alamein, British forces, equipped with advanced tanks and aided by superior intelligence, were able to halt the Axis advance into Egypt. The battle marked a turning point in the North African campaign, showcasing the importance of combined arms tactics, where tanks, artillery, and air support worked together effectively.

Kursk, fought in July 1943, was the largest tank battle in history and a significant Soviet victory. The Germans launched Operation Citadel, intending to encircle Soviet forces and regain the initiative on the Eastern Front. However, the Soviets had prepared extensive defenses, and their tank forces, including the T-34 and the newly developed IS-2 heavy tank, were ready to counter the German assault. The battle underscored the importance of intelligence, preparation, and the ability to adapt tactics to the evolving battlefield conditions.

The introduction of specialized tank units, such as the Soviet's Guards Tank Armies and the German Panzer Divisions, further emphasized the strategic significance of armored warfare. These units were trained and equipped to exploit breakthroughs in enemy lines, encircling and destroying opposing forces. The mobility and firepower of tanks allowed for rapid advances into enemy territory, contributing to the overall strategy of encirclement and destruction that characterized much of World War II.

Ultimately, the dominance of tanks in land battles during World War II reshaped military doctrine for generations to come. The lessons learned from these armored engagements influenced post-war military strategies, leading to continued innovation in tank design and tactics. The tank's capacity to deliver firepower, mobility, and protection firmly established it as a cornerstone of modern warfare, demonstrating its critical role in shaping the outcome of World War II. As military historians reflect on this period, the tank battles of WWII serve as a testament to the transformative power of armored warfare and its enduring legacy in military history.

Air Superiority

The Second World War marked a pivotal moment in military history, where air power emerged as a decisive factor in determining the outcomes of conflicts. The development and strategic use of aircraft transformed traditional warfare, facilitating rapid advancements in tactics that underscored the importance of achieving air superiority.

At the onset of WWII, air power was recognized for its potential to influence ground and naval operations dramatically. The Luftwaffe, Germany's air force, demonstrated the effectiveness of strategic bombing campaigns during the Blitzkrieg (lightning war) tactics that combined fast-moving ground forces with coordinated air strikes. This approach not only disrupted enemy supply lines but also demoralized civilian populations, effectively crippling the enemy's will to resist. The swift victories in Poland and France showcased the effectiveness of air superiority in supporting ground troops and seizing control of the battlefield.

One of the most significant aspects of air power during WWII was the development of advanced aircraft technologies. Fighters like the Supermarine Spitfire and the North American P-51 Mustang were designed for speed, agility, and firepower. These aircraft became instrumental in engaging enemy bombers and fighters, ensuring control over the skies. The Battle of Britain in 1940 epitomized this struggle for air supremacy, as the Royal Air Force defended against the Luftwaffe's onslaught. The successful defense not only thwarted German plans for invasion but also established the crucial role of air power in protecting national sovereignty.

As the war progressed, the strategic bombing campaign became a cornerstone of Allied military strategy. The Allied forces employed heavy bombers like the B-17 Flying Fortress and the B-29 Superfortress to conduct large-scale bombing raids over Germany and Japan. These operations aimed to destroy industrial capabilities, transportation networks, and military targets, thereby crippling the enemy's ability to sustain war efforts. The bombing of cities such as Dresden and Tokyo highlighted the devastating impact of air power on civilian infrastructure and morale, signaling a shift toward total war where civilian and military targets were indistinguishable.

Naval aviation also transformed maritime warfare during WWII. Aircraft carriers emerged as the central vessels in naval fleets, replacing battleships as the primary means of projecting power at sea. The attack on Pearl Harbor exemplified the effectiveness of carrier-based aircraft in launching surprise assaults against enemy naval forces. Subsequently, naval battles in the Pacific, such as the Battle of Midway, showcased the strategic importance of air superiority in naval engagements, where carrier-based planes played decisive roles in sinking enemy ships and altering the course of battles.

Moreover, the advent of new technologies, such as radar and long-range bombers, further emphasized the tactical evolution of air warfare. Radar allowed for early detection of enemy aircraft, providing a critical edge in defensive operations. The introduction of long-range bombers facilitated strategic bombing campaigns that could reach deep into enemy territory, making air power an integral component of military strategy.

The impact of air power during WWII extended beyond immediate military victories; it reshaped post-war military doctrines. The lessons learned in aerial warfare led to the understanding that control of the air was essential for successful ground and naval operations in future conflicts. The legacy of WWII solidified the belief that air superiority was not merely an auxiliary component of warfare but a fundamental requirement for achieving victory.

In conclusion, the role of aircraft in WWII was transformative, highlighting the significance of air superiority in modern warfare. The integration of advanced aircraft technologies, strategic bombing campaigns, and naval aviation underscored the necessity of controlling the skies to ensure success on the ground and at sea. The Second World War established air power as a decisive factor that would continue to influence military strategies long after the conflict ended, paving the way for the future of aerial warfare.

Naval Warfare in WWII

World War II marked a significant evolution in naval warfare, characterized by the strategic development and deployment of submarines, aircraft carriers, and battleships. Each type of vessel played a pivotal role in shaping naval strategies and outcomes across various theaters of war, particularly in the Atlantic and Pacific Oceans.

The Rise of Submarines

Submarines, particularly those utilized by Germany, the United States, and Japan, became formidable tools of warfare during WWII. The German U-boat campaign aimed at disrupting Allied shipping lanes was a key strategy that sought to starve Britain into submission. The effectiveness of U-boats was underscored by their ability to attack merchant vessels and military supply ships without warning, leading to significant losses for the Allies in the early years of the war.

The technological advancements in submarine design—including improved stealth capabilities, longer ranges, and more effective torpedoes—enhanced their operational efficiency. The introduction of the "wolf pack" tactic, where groups of U-boats coordinated attacks on convoys, exemplified the strategic shift towards more aggressive submarine warfare. The Allies responded with innovations such as depth charges and sonar technology, ultimately leading to the decline of U-boat effectiveness as the war progressed.

Aircraft Carriers: The New Capital Ships

The introduction and prominence of aircraft carriers during WWII represented a revolutionary shift in naval power dynamics. Unlike traditional battleships, which dominated previous naval engagements, aircraft carriers allowed for the projection of air power over vast distances. The carrier became the centerpiece of naval strategy, enabling fleets to engage enemies without direct confrontation at sea.

The pivotal Battle of Midway in 1942 showcased the strategic importance of aircraft carriers. In a decisive victory for the United States, carrier-based aircraft sank four Japanese carriers, altering the balance of power in the Pacific. This battle highlighted the transition from battleship-to-carrier dominance, as the ability to launch airstrikes from a distance proved to be more effective in engaging enemy forces.

The evolution of carrier technology, including advancements in aircraft design, radar systems, and onboard operations, enabled fleets to conduct extensive air operations, including reconnaissance, ground support, and anti-ship attacks. Aircraft carriers became the primary tool for power projection, leading to the development of "fast carriers" that could quickly respond to threats across the vast expanses of ocean.

Battleships: The Last of Their Kind

Despite the rise of submarines and aircraft carriers, battleships remained integral to naval warfare during WWII, particularly in the early years of the conflict. Battleships like the USS Missouri and the Japanese Yamato were equipped with massive guns capable of delivering devastating firepower. Their role in shore bombardment and fleet engagements remained significant, especially in battles such as the Battle of the Atlantic and the naval engagements in the Pacific.

However, the vulnerability of battleships to air attacks became evident as the war progressed. The sinking of the battleship Prince of Wales by Japanese aircraft in 1941 underscored the shift in naval warfare priorities. As aircraft carriers rose to prominence, battleships began to be viewed as less essential in fleet actions, leading to a gradual decline in their construction and deployment.

Conclusion

The evolution of naval warfare during World War II was marked by the strategic integration of submarines, aircraft carriers, and battleships, each contributing uniquely to the conflict. Submarines introduced a new dimension of stealth and surprise, while aircraft carriers redefined naval power projection and air dominance. Battleships, though still formidable, faced obsolescence as air power became the predominant force at sea. This transformation not only dictated the strategies employed during WWII but also set the stage for future naval engagements in the post-war era, where the lessons learned from this conflict would shape naval doctrine for decades to come.

The Manhattan Project

The Manhattan Project, a monumental and secretive endeavor during World War II, marked a pivotal moment in the history of weaponry and warfare. Conceived in response to fears that Nazi Germany might develop nuclear weapons first, the project brought together some of the greatest scientific minds of the time, including physicists J. Robert Oppenheimer, Enrico Fermi, and Richard Feynman, among others. The project was not merely a military initiative; it represented a significant fusion of science, engineering, and military strategy, culminating in the development of the first nuclear weapons.

Initiated in 1942, the Manhattan Project aimed to harness the energy released from nuclear fission—the splitting of atomic nuclei—to create a bomb of unprecedented destructive power. The project was conducted across several sites in the United States, including Los Alamos, Oak Ridge, and Hanford, each specializing in different aspects of nuclear research and production. The collaborative efforts of scientists, engineers, and military personnel facilitated rapid advancements in nuclear physics and engineering, leading to the successful detonation of the first atomic bomb during the Trinity Test in New Mexico on July 16, 1945.

The successful detonation of the bomb had profound implications for warfare. The atomic bomb was a game-changer, as it introduced a new dimension of military power that was not only capable of annihilating vast numbers of people but also could alter the strategic calculations of nations. On August 6 and 9, 1945, the United States dropped atomic bombs on the Japanese cities of Hiroshima and Nagasaki, leading to catastrophic loss of life and unprecedented destruction. This marked not only the end of World War II but also the beginning of the nuclear age.

The immediate effects of the bombings were staggering. Hiroshima suffered an estimated 140,000 deaths by the end of 1945, while Nagasaki saw around 74,000 fatalities. The bombs caused immense physical destruction, obliterating entire cities and leaving survivors to contend with severe injuries, radiation sickness, and long-term health consequences. The ethical implications of using such a weapon were hotly debated, raising questions about the morality of targeting civilians and the justification for using such a devastating force to end the war.

Strategically, the existence of nuclear weapons transformed international relations and military doctrine. The concept of deterrence became central to Cold War strategy, as nations sought to prevent conflict through the threat of mutually assured destruction (MAD). The fear of nuclear war influenced military planning, diplomacy, and even domestic policies. Countries with nuclear capabilities became acutely aware that the stakes of conflict had risen dramatically, as a conventional war could easily escalate into a nuclear confrontation.

The Manhattan Project also set the stage for a global arms race, as nations scrambled to develop their own nuclear arsenals. The post-war era saw the proliferation of nuclear weapons technology, leading to a complex web of treaties and agreements aimed at controlling and regulating nuclear arms. The Non-Proliferation Treaty (NPT), established in 1968, sought to prevent the spread of nuclear weapons and promote disarmament, reflecting the ongoing struggle to balance security with the ethical implications of nuclear warfare.

In summary, the Manhattan Project not only led to the development of nuclear weapons but fundamentally altered the nature of warfare and international relations. The advent of atomic bombs created a new paradigm in military strategy, underscoring the necessity for diplomacy and arms control in an increasingly dangerous world. As we continue to grapple with the legacy of nuclear technology, the lessons learned from the Manhattan Project remain crucial in navigating the complexities of modern warfare and global security.

Chapter 12

The Cold War and the Nuclear Arms Race

The Dawn of the Nuclear Age

The dawn of the nuclear age was marked by the bombings of Hiroshima and Nagasaki in August 1945, two pivotal events that not only concluded World War II but also reshaped the geopolitical landscape of the post-war world. The atomic bombings revealed the devastating power of nuclear weapons and initiated a profound transformation in international relations, military strategy, and the balance of power among nations.

On August 6, 1945, the United States dropped the first atomic bomb, codenamed "Little Boy," on Hiroshima, a city with significant military and industrial importance. The immediate destruction was catastrophic: approximately 140,000 people were killed by the end of the year, with many more suffering from injuries and radiation sickness. Just three days later, on August 9, the U.S. dropped a second bomb, "Fat Man," on Nagasaki, resulting in about 70,000 deaths. The sheer destructiveness of these weapons, capable of obliterating entire cities in an instant, sent shockwaves throughout the world.

The bombings of Hiroshima and Nagasaki served as a stark demonstration of the consequences of nuclear warfare, instilling fear and urgency in global politics. The sheer scale of destruction not only forced Japan to surrender, thus ending WWII, but also positioned the United States as a dominant military power with unprecedented capabilities. This newfound power fundamentally altered the dynamics of international relations, initiating the era of nuclear deterrence.

In the aftermath of the bombings, a global arms race ensued as nations scrambled to develop their own nuclear arsenals. The Soviet Union, in particular, viewed the U.S. monopoly on nuclear weapons as a direct threat to its security and influence. This fear spurred the Soviet Union to accelerate its nuclear program, culminating in its first successful atomic test in 1949. The subsequent development of more advanced weapons, including hydrogen bombs, further intensified tensions between the two superpowers.

The notion of mutually assured destruction (MAD) emerged during this period, positing that the possession of nuclear weapons by both the U.S. and the Soviet Union would deter either side from initiating a conflict. This doctrine was underpinned by the understanding that any nuclear exchange would result in catastrophic consequences for both parties. As a result, the Cold War was characterized by a precarious balance of power, where the threat of nuclear annihilation loomed large over global politics.

The bombings also had profound implications for international law and ethics. The unprecedented suffering experienced by the civilian populations of Hiroshima and Nagasaki prompted an urgent reevaluation of the moral and humanitarian dimensions of warfare. The use of atomic bombs led to widespread debates regarding the legitimacy of nuclear weapons, their impact on civilian populations, and the ethical responsibilities of nations engaged in warfare. This discourse influenced the development of international treaties aimed at controlling the proliferation of nuclear weapons, such as the Treaty on the Non-Proliferation of Nuclear Weapons (NPT), established in 1968.

Moreover, the bombings catalyzed movements advocating for nuclear disarmament, as voices emerged calling for the global community to confront the ethical dilemmas posed by the existence of such devastating weapons. The memory of Hiroshima and Nagasaki has been enshrined in cultural narratives, shaping public perception and influencing policy debates regarding nuclear weapons.

In conclusion, the dawn of the nuclear age, marked by the bombings of Hiroshima and Nagasaki, fundamentally altered the trajectory of global geopolitics. The immediate impact of these events reshaped military strategies, initiated an arms race, and prompted critical ethical discussions on warfare and humanity. As the world grapples with the ongoing implications of nuclear weapons, the legacy of Hiroshima and Nagasaki serves as a poignant reminder of the need for vigilance in the pursuit of peace and disarmament in an age defined by the potential for catastrophic destruction.

The Arms Race

The nuclear arms race between the United States and the Soviet Union during the Cold War represented one of the most significant and perilous periods in modern history. This competition was driven not only by the desire for military superiority but also by ideological differences and the quest for global influence. The quest to develop and stockpile nuclear weapons fundamentally altered international relations and created a precarious balance of power known as Mutually Assured Destruction (MAD).

The origins of the nuclear arms race can be traced back to World War II, when the United States successfully developed the atomic bomb under the Manhattan Project. The bombing of Hiroshima and Nagasaki in August 1945 demonstrated the devastating power of nuclear weapons, marking the United States as the first nation to wield this unprecedented military capability. However, the Soviet Union quickly recognized the implications of this new era of warfare and began its own nuclear program in response.

In 1949, the Soviet Union successfully tested its first atomic bomb, known as "Joe 1," effectively ending the United States' monopoly on nuclear weapons. This event triggered a sense of urgency within the U.S. government, leading to increased funding and emphasis on nuclear research and development. The competition intensified as both superpowers sought to enhance their arsenals, leading to the development of more advanced weapons systems.

The U.S. initially focused on the hydrogen bomb, a far more powerful weapon than the atomic bomb, which was successfully tested in November 1952. The Soviet Union followed suit, detonating its hydrogen bomb the following year. This marked a pivotal moment in the arms race, as both nations now possessed weapons that could cause catastrophic destruction on a scale previously unimaginable.

The concept of MAD emerged during this period, rooted in the understanding that both superpowers could inflict unacceptable damage on one another. This tenuous balance created an environment where neither side could afford to strike first without facing devastating retaliation. Consequently, the arms race became a contest not only of technological superiority but also of psychological strategy.

Throughout the 1950s and 1960s, the race continued to escalate, with both nations developing a variety of delivery systems, including intercontinental ballistic missiles (ICBMs), submarine-launched ballistic missiles (SLBMs), and strategic bombers. The introduction of ICBMs allowed for rapid, long-range attacks, fundamentally changing the nature of nuclear deterrence. The Soviet Union and the U.S. engaged in a series of tests and counter-tests, with each nation attempting to outpace the other in both quantity and sophistication of its nuclear arsenal.

This arms race extended beyond mere numbers; it also encompassed a race for technological advancements. The development of missile defense systems, early warning systems, and second-strike capabilities became critical elements in the strategic calculus of both superpowers. The Cuban Missile Crisis in 1962 highlighted the dangers of this competition, bringing the world to the brink of nuclear war and underscoring the volatile nature of the arms race.

As the Cold War continued into the 1970s and 1980s, both the U.S. and the Soviet Union recognized the unsustainable nature of their nuclear buildup. Diplomatic efforts led to a series of arms control agreements, such as the Strategic Arms Limitation Talks (SALT) and later the Intermediate-Range Nuclear Forces Treaty (INF), which sought to limit the proliferation of nuclear weapons and reduce the risk of accidental conflict.

In summary, the arms race between the United States and the Soviet Union was characterized by rapid advancements in nuclear technology and a relentless pursuit of military dominance.

The legacy of this period continues to shape international relations and discussions around nuclear non-proliferation and disarmament, highlighting the enduring impact of this critical chapter in the history of weaponry. As nations grapple with the implications of nuclear arsenals, the lessons learned from the Cold War remain relevant in addressing the complexities of modern security challenges.

The Role of Ballistic Missiles and Delivery Systems

The development of ballistic missiles and their associated delivery systems has been one of the most significant advancements in military technology since the mid-20th century. This evolution not only transformed military strategy but also had profound implications for global security dynamics, particularly during the Cold War era.

Origins and Early Developments

The origins of ballistic missile technology can be traced back to the V-2 rocket developed by Nazi Germany during World War II. This was the world's first long-range guided ballistic missile, capable of delivering payloads over vast distances. The war spurred significant advancements in rocket technology, laying the groundwork for post-war missile development by both the United States and the Soviet Union.

After World War II, the geopolitical landscape shifted dramatically, and the arms race intensified. The U.S. and the Soviet Union embarked on a quest to develop more advanced missile systems that could deliver nuclear warheads, fundamentally altering the nature of warfare. The development of Intercontinental Ballistic Missiles (ICBMs) in the 1950s marked a pivotal point in military strategy. These missiles, capable of traveling thousands of miles and reaching targets in a matter of minutes, brought the concept of mutually assured destruction (MAD) into the forefront of military doctrine.

Impact on Military Strategy

Ballistic missiles changed the dynamics of warfare by introducing a new strategic deterrent. The ability to launch a nuclear strike from a land-based silo or a mobile platform created a deterrent effect that shaped international relations. Countries recognized that the threat of mutually assured destruction would prevent direct military confrontations between nuclear powers, leading to a tense stability known as the Cold War.

The development of Submarine-Launched Ballistic Missiles (SLBMs) further enhanced this deterrent capability. By deploying missiles on submarines, nations could ensure second-strike capability, making it exceedingly difficult for an adversary to eliminate their nuclear arsenal in a preemptive strike. This diversification of delivery systems added layers of complexity to military planning and increased the stakes of escalation.

Technological Advancements and Challenges

The arms race prompted rapid technological advancements in missile design, accuracy, and payload capabilities. The introduction of Multiple Independently Targetable Reentry Vehicles (MIRVs) allowed a single missile to carry several warheads, each capable of striking different targets. This increased the destructive potential of a single missile launch and complicated missile defense strategies, as intercepting multiple warheads became a daunting challenge.

However, the proliferation of missile technology also raised significant security concerns. The spread of ballistic missile technology to non-nuclear states and non-state actors presented new challenges for international security. Countries like North Korea and Iran have pursued ballistic missile programs that raised alarms in the international community, leading to diplomatic tensions and sanctions.

Conclusion: The Ongoing Arms Race

The role of ballistic missiles and their delivery systems in the arms race illustrates the dual nature of technological advancement in warfare. While these systems have provided nations with unprecedented deterrence capabilities, they have also escalated the risks of conflict and miscalculation. The ongoing evolution of missile technology, including the development of hypersonic glide vehicles and advanced defensive systems, continues to shape military strategies and international relations.

In essence, ballistic missiles represent a critical intersection of technology, strategy, and global security. Their impact extends beyond mere military utility, influencing diplomatic relations, arms control negotiations, and the very fabric of international peace and stability. As nations grapple with emerging technologies and their implications for warfare, the legacy of ballistic missiles will undoubtedly continue to shape the future of global security.

Proxy Wars

The Cold War, a prolonged period of geopolitical tension between the United States and the Soviet Union from the late 1940s to the early 1990s, was characterized by a complex web of conflicts where both superpowers sought to expand their influence without engaging in direct military confrontation. One of the most significant aspects of this era was the phenomenon of proxy wars, where the two powers supported opposing sides in regional conflicts using conventional weapons. This strategy allowed them to indirectly engage one another while minimizing the risk of a full-scale nuclear war.

Two notable examples of proxy wars during the Cold War are the Korean War (1950-1953) and the Vietnam War (1955-1975). In these conflicts, conventional weapons played a crucial role, shaping the strategies and outcomes of the battles fought.

The Korean War

The Korean War emerged from the division of Korea after World War II, with the North backed by the Soviet Union and China, while the South received support from the United States and other Western allies. The conflict was marked by significant conventional warfare, where both sides utilized infantry, tanks, artillery, and air power in large-scale operations.

The United States employed its military technology and conventional weapons extensively throughout the Korean War. American forces utilized advanced aircraft like the F-86 Sabre and bombers such as the B-29 Superfortress, which were pivotal in achieving air superiority. Ground troops relied on a variety of infantry weapons, including the M1 Garand rifle and Browning Automatic Rifle (BAR), providing them with the firepower necessary to engage North Korean and Chinese forces.

On the other side, North Korean and Chinese forces used Soviet-supplied weapons, including the T-34 tank and the PPSh-41 submachine gun. The conflict showcased the effectiveness of conventional military hardware in a modern warfare context, leading to high casualties on both sides and a stalemate that resulted in the division of Korea along the 38th parallel.

The Vietnam War

The Vietnam War represents another significant proxy conflict where conventional weapons were utilized extensively. The United States intervened in Vietnam to support the South Vietnamese government against the communist Viet Cong and North Vietnamese forces. The war escalated in the 1960s and became a contentious issue in American society, leading to widespread protests.

American military strategy in Vietnam relied heavily on conventional weaponry, including the M16 rifle, artillery, and helicopter gunships like the Bell AH-1 Cobra and the CH-47 Chinook. Air power was a critical component, with the U.S. conducting extensive bombing campaigns using aircraft such as the F-4 Phantom II and dropping bombs like the infamous Napalm to destroy enemy positions and infrastructure.

Conversely, North Vietnamese forces employed a mix of conventional and guerrilla warfare tactics. They utilized Soviet-supplied weaponry, such as the AK-47 assault rifle, and relied on the Ho Chi Minh Trail for logistics. The conflict highlighted the challenges of conventional warfare when faced with asymmetric tactics, as the Viet Cong utilized their knowledge of the terrain to launch ambushes and utilize traps, undermining the effectiveness of more advanced American equipment.

Conclusion

The proxy wars of the Cold War exemplified the strategic use of conventional weapons as tools of influence and power projection. Both the Korean and Vietnam Wars illustrated the complexities of modern warfare, where the superpowers sought to assert their ideologies and geopolitical interests through indirect means. The extensive use of conventional weapons led to significant military engagements and highlighted the challenges of fighting in diverse environments against unconventional tactics. These conflicts not only shaped the military strategies of the Cold War era but also had profound implications for international relations and military doctrine in the subsequent decades.

The Threat of Mutually Assured Destruction (MAD) and Its Influence on Cold War Strategy

Mutually Assured Destruction (MAD) emerged as a pivotal doctrine during the Cold War, fundamentally shaping the strategic calculus of the United States and the Soviet Union. The concept is based on the premise that if two opposing sides possess enough nuclear weapons to destroy each other completely, the certainty of total annihilation acts as a deterrent against the actual use of those weapons. This delicate equilibrium of terror maintained peace through fear rather than through diplomacy or traditional military engagements.

The genesis of MAD can be traced back to the late 1940s and early 1950s, following the atomic bombings of Hiroshima and Nagasaki in 1945. The devastating power of nuclear weapons became apparent, leading both superpowers to amass vast arsenals. By the 1960s, the United States and the Soviet Union were locked in a nuclear arms race, each striving to outdo the other in the quantity and sophistication of their nuclear capabilities. The doctrine of MAD was thus born from the necessity of ensuring that neither side would initiate a nuclear conflict, knowing that such an action would result in their own destruction.

MAD relied on a few critical components: the development of a second-strike capability, a robust and survivable nuclear arsenal, and the establishment of credible deterrence mechanisms. The second-strike capability meant that even if one side was attacked first, it would still possess enough nuclear weapons to retaliate effectively, ensuring that the aggressor would face catastrophic consequences. This concept was vital for maintaining the credibility of deterrence, as it prevented either side from considering a preemptive nuclear strike.

The strategic triad, comprising land-based intercontinental ballistic missiles (ICBMs), submarine-launched ballistic missiles (SLBMs), and strategic bombers, was a cornerstone of U.S. nuclear policy. This diversification of delivery systems ensured that no single attack could eliminate the entire nuclear arsenal of the United States. The Soviet Union, in turn, developed similar capabilities, leading to a precarious balance of power.

The influence of MAD on Cold War strategy extended beyond mere military posturing. It permeated political, social, and cultural dimensions, shaping public perception and policy decisions. The fear of nuclear war became a defining characteristic of the era, leading to widespread anti-nuclear movements and calls for disarmament. Films, literature, and art from the period often grappled with themes of existential dread and the absurdity of a world living under the shadow of nuclear annihilation.

MAD also had implications for international relations and alliances. NATO and the Warsaw Pact were formed during this period, with each side relying on nuclear deterrence as a means of ensuring collective security. The doctrine influenced numerous crises, including the Cuban Missile Crisis in 1962, when the world teetered on the brink of nuclear war. The successful resolution of that crisis reinforced the efficacy of MAD, as both superpowers recognized the catastrophic consequences of nuclear engagement.

However, while MAD effectively deterred direct conflict between the superpowers, it did not eliminate the risk of miscalculations or accidents. The doctrine created an environment where any perceived threat could escalate rapidly, with both sides operating under a hair-trigger alert status. This paradox of deterrence underscored the fragile nature of global security during the Cold War.

In conclusion, the concept of Mutually Assured Destruction was instrumental in defining the strategic landscape of the Cold War. By establishing a precarious balance of terror, it served as both a deterrent to nuclear war and a source of profound anxiety for humanity. The legacy of MAD continues to influence discussions on nuclear policy and international security, as the world grapples with the challenges of proliferation and the ever-present threat of nuclear conflict. As such, understanding MAD is essential for comprehending not only the Cold War era but also the ongoing complexities of global security in a nuclear age.

Chapter 13

Post-Cold War and Modern Warfare

The Evolution of Precision-Guided Munitions

The evolution of precision-guided munitions (PGMs) marks one of the most significant advancements in military technology, transforming the landscape of warfare from the mid-20th century onwards. These sophisticated weapons, often referred to as "smart weapons," utilize advanced guidance systems that allow them to strike targets with unprecedented accuracy, minimizing collateral damage and increasing operational effectiveness.

Historical Context

The origins of PGMs can be traced back to World War II, where early attempts at guided weaponry included the German V-1 and V-2 rockets, which laid the groundwork for future developments. However, it wasn't until the Vietnam War that the concept of precision-guided munitions gained prominence. The introduction of laser-guided bombs, notably the GBU-10 and GBU-12, allowed for more accurate strikes on enemy fortifications and infrastructure, showcasing the potential to reduce civilian casualties and enhance mission success rates.

Technological Advancements

The evolution of PGMs has been driven by significant advancements in technology. The integration of global positioning systems (GPS) in the late 20th century revolutionized the design and functionality of munitions. GPS-guided bombs, such as the Joint Direct Attack Munition (JDAM), can be launched from great distances and still achieve pinpoint accuracy. This ability to strike moving or stationary targets with exceptional precision has fundamentally altered military strategies, allowing forces to engage high-value targets with minimal risk to surrounding areas.

Moreover, advancements in guidance systems have diversified the types of PGMs available. Today, munitions can utilize a combination of guidance technologies, including laser guidance, inertial navigation, and satellite guidance, enhancing their effectiveness across various combat scenarios. The development of smart missiles, such as the AGM-86 ALCM and the Tomahawk cruise missile, exemplifies this evolution, providing military forces with the capability to strike targets deep within enemy territory while minimizing exposure to air defenses.

Impact on Warfare

The introduction and widespread use of PGMs have had profound implications for modern warfare. One of the most significant changes has been the shift in airpower strategy. Air forces now prioritize precision over sheer quantity, allowing for rapid, targeted strikes that can disrupt enemy operations with minimal risk to civilians. This shift has also influenced ground operations, as ground troops can call in precision airstrikes to support their missions, effectively integrating air and ground capabilities.

Additionally, the operational flexibility afforded by PGMs has transformed the nature of conflicts. The ability to conduct precision strikes has enabled militaries to engage in limited warfare, where the focus is on specific tactical objectives rather than large-scale destruction. This approach is particularly evident in conflicts such as the Gulf War and the War on Terror, where precision-guided munitions were essential in targeting insurgents and terrorist networks while avoiding collateral damage.

Ethical Considerations and Challenges

While PGMs have enhanced operational effectiveness, their use also raises ethical and legal questions. The notion of "surgical strikes" can create a false sense of security regarding collateral damage, as even precision weapons can inadvertently harm civilians, particularly in urban environments. Moreover, the reliance on technology introduces vulnerabilities, such as cyber threats that could potentially compromise guidance systems.

As militaries continue to develop and deploy PGMs, the need for robust international regulations governing their use becomes increasingly urgent. Ensuring accountability and adherence to humanitarian laws is essential in maintaining the moral high ground in warfare.

Conclusion

The evolution of precision-guided munitions has fundamentally reshaped the battlefield, enabling militaries to achieve strategic objectives with remarkable accuracy and reduced collateral damage. As technology continues to advance, the future of PGMs will likely involve further innovations, including autonomous systems and enhanced targeting capabilities. However, the ethical implications of their use must be carefully considered to balance military efficacy with humanitarian concerns. As the nature of warfare evolves, so too will the role of precision-guided munitions in shaping military operations and strategies.

The Role of Drones in Modern Combat

Unmanned Aerial Vehicles (UAVs), commonly known as drones, have revolutionized modern combat, fundamentally altering the landscape of military operations. Their rise represents not just a technological evolution but a paradigm shift in how warfare is conducted. Drones are now integral to surveillance, reconnaissance, and offensive operations, providing military forces with capabilities that were previously unimaginable.

Evolution and Technology

The development of drones began during the early 20th century, but it was not until the late 20th and early 21st centuries that technological advancements in sensors, communications, and materials allowed for the widespread deployment of UAVs in military operations. Modern drones are equipped with sophisticated technology, including high-resolution cameras, infrared sensors, and advanced navigation systems, enabling them to conduct long-range missions with high precision. Notably, the introduction of systems like the MQ-1 Predator and MQ-9 Reaper showcased drones' potential for both intelligence-gathering and targeted strikes, blurring the lines between traditional airpower and ground forces.

Strategic Advantages

One of the most significant advantages of drones is their ability to operate in environments that are too dangerous for manned aircraft. Drones can loiter over hostile territory for extended periods, gathering intelligence and conducting surveillance without risking the lives of pilots. This capability has been particularly useful in counterterrorism operations, where drones can track and target insurgents in remote locations, often with real-time data transmission to command centers.

Moreover, drones have drastically reduced the time it takes to gather intelligence and execute strikes. The ability to conduct real-time analysis of footage and relay this information back to military planners enhances situational awareness and decision-making processes. This immediacy can be crucial in fast-paced combat scenarios where traditional reconnaissance methods may lag.

Ethical Considerations

The use of drones in warfare also raises significant ethical and legal questions. The detachment of operators from the battlefield creates a psychological distance that can lead to controversial decisions regarding the use of lethal force. Critics argue that drone strikes can result in civilian casualties and may violate international law. The concept of "signature strikes," where targets are identified based on patterns of behavior rather than confirmed identities, has sparked intense debate regarding the morality of such operations.

Additionally, the proliferation of drone technology has led to concerns about accountability. As more nations and non-state actors acquire UAVs, the potential for misuse increases, raising fears about their application in conflicts and terrorism.

Future Implications

As military technology continues to evolve, the role of drones is likely to expand further. Future UAVs may incorporate artificial intelligence, enabling autonomous decision-making in combat situations. This shift could enhance operational efficiency but also deepens the ethical dilemmas associated with autonomous weapons systems.

Furthermore, the integration of drones with other military assets—such as cyber warfare capabilities and ground robots—will create a more comprehensive approach to modern combat. This interconnectedness will enable armed forces to conduct coordinated multi-domain operations, enhancing their effectiveness on the battlefield.

Conclusion

In summary, drones have established themselves as pivotal tools in modern military operations, offering unique capabilities that enhance both strategic planning and tactical execution. However, their use is fraught with ethical and legal challenges that must be addressed to ensure responsible application. As technology progresses, the continuing evolution of drones will likely shape the future of warfare, presenting both opportunities and challenges for military strategy and international security. The balance between leveraging these advanced technologies and adhering to ethical standards will be a defining factor in the ongoing discourse surrounding modern combat.

Cyber Warfare

In the ever-evolving landscape of modern warfare, cyber warfare has emerged as a significant and transformative element. The proliferation of digital technologies and the internet has not only reshaped the way nations communicate and conduct business but has also redefined the strategies and tactics employed in conflicts. Cyber warfare pertains to the use of digital attacks by one nation to disrupt the vital computer systems of another, thereby inflicting damage, stealing sensitive information, or even causing physical destruction. Unlike traditional warfare, which relies on physical weapons and military forces, cyber warfare operates in the virtual realm, often remaining hidden from the public eye until significant damage is done.

The roots of cyber warfare can be traced back to the late 20th century, coinciding with the rise of the internet and the growing interconnectivity of computer systems. The U.S. Department of Defense, recognizing the potential of cyber operations, began to develop strategies for offensive and defensive cyber capabilities. Events such as the 2007 cyberattacks on Estonia, where government, media, and financial websites were incapacitated, underscored the vulnerabilities that nations face in an increasingly cyber-dependent world. This incident marked a significant turning point, demonstrating that cyberattacks could be utilized as tools of political coercion and warfare.

In contemporary conflicts, cyber warfare serves multiple purposes. It can be used to gather intelligence, disrupt enemy operations, or undermine public trust in government institutions. For instance, during the 2016 U.S. presidential election, cyberattacks attributed to Russian operatives aimed at compromising the electoral process and influencing public perception. These attacks not only targeted political organizations but also spread misinformation on social media platforms, illustrating the multifaceted nature of modern cyber warfare. The potential for cyber operations to influence public opinion and disrupt democratic processes raises profound questions about sovereignty and security in the digital age.

One of the most alarming aspects of cyber warfare is its potential for collateral damage. Unlike conventional weapons that target specific military installations, cyberattacks can inadvertently affect civilian infrastructures, such as hospitals, power grids, and transportation systems. The 2017 WannaCry ransomware attack, which affected hundreds of thousands of computers across the globe, including critical healthcare systems in the UK, showcased the indiscriminate nature of cyber threats. Such incidents highlight the urgent need for robust cybersecurity measures to protect both military and civilian assets from potential attacks.

Moreover, the anonymity offered by the internet complicates the attribution of cyberattacks. Unlike traditional warfare, where the aggressor can often be identified, cyber operations can be shrouded in ambiguity. This uncertainty can lead to escalation as nations grapple with how to respond to perceived threats while avoiding miscalculations that could lead to open conflict. The lack of established norms and rules governing cyber warfare further adds to the complexity, as nations navigate this new frontier with varying degrees of understanding and preparedness.

As technology continues to advance, the tools and tactics of cyber warfare will likely evolve. The integration of artificial intelligence and machine learning into cyber operations can enhance both offensive and defensive capabilities, allowing for more sophisticated attacks and quicker responses. Nations are increasingly investing in developing cyber capabilities, resulting in a global arms race in the digital domain.

In conclusion, cyber warfare represents a new frontier in the landscape of modern conflict, challenging traditional notions of warfare and security. As nations become more dependent on technology, the implications of cyber operations will only grow in significance. The need for international cooperation in establishing norms, regulations, and preventive measures against cyber threats has never been more crucial as the world grapples with the complexities and dangers of this new dimension of warfare.

The Continued Role of Conventional Weapons

Despite the rise of advanced technologies in warfare, such as drones, cyber warfare capabilities, and precision-guided munitions, conventional weapons—those traditionally used in combat—continue to play a crucial role in modern conflicts. This persistence is evident across various theaters of war, where rifles, artillery, and other classic armaments maintain their significance for several reasons.

1. Accessibility and Affordability:

One of the most compelling reasons for the continued reliance on conventional weapons is their accessibility. Many nations, especially those with limited defense budgets, can procure conventional arms at a fraction of the cost of high-tech systems. For example, while advanced aircraft and missile systems require substantial investment in technology and maintenance, conventional firearms and artillery pieces can often be produced locally or purchased from surplus stocks. This affordability allows smaller states and non-state actors to equip their forces adequately, making conventional weapons a staple in both national militaries and insurgent groups.

2. Simplicity and Reliability:

Conventional weapons are often simpler in design and use compared to their modern counterparts. For instance, bolt-action rifles and basic artillery systems do not require extensive training or complex logistical support. During conflicts where rapid deployment and immediate action are necessary, the reliability of conventional arms can outweigh the benefits of more sophisticated technologies. Moreover, in environments where high-tech systems may fail due to electronic jamming or a lack of maintenance, traditional weaponry often proves more dependable.

3. Versatility in Various Combat Scenarios:

Conventional weapons have demonstrated their versatility across diverse combat scenarios. In urban warfare, for instance, the close-quarters nature of fighting often favors firearms such as assault rifles, shotguns, and sidearms due to their maneuverability and effectiveness in confined spaces. Similarly, artillery continues to provide crucial support in both offensive and defensive operations, capable of delivering firepower over long distances to suppress enemy positions or fortifications.

4. Integration with Modern Tactics:

Modern military strategies frequently incorporate conventional weapons alongside advanced technologies, creating a hybrid approach to warfare. For example, infantry units equipped with rifles and machine guns often work in conjunction with drones for reconnaissance and targeting, leveraging the strengths of both conventional and modern weaponry. This integration enhances operational effectiveness, allowing forces to adapt to various combat conditions while still relying on proven conventional arms.

5. The Role of Conventional Weapons in Asymmetrical Warfare:

In contemporary conflicts characterized by asymmetrical warfare, traditional weaponry often becomes the equalizer for less technologically advanced forces. Non-state actors and insurgent groups frequently utilize conventional arms to mount effective resistance against more equipped adversaries. The enduring presence of rifles, grenades, and improvised explosive devices (IEDs) in such conflicts underlines the adaptability and relevance of conventional weaponry in modern combat.

6. Cultural and Psychological Factors:

Beyond practical considerations, cultural and psychological factors also contribute to the continued relevance of conventional weapons. For many military traditions, conventional arms symbolize honor and bravery. They are often used in ceremonial roles and maintain a place in the collective consciousness of armed forces around the world. Furthermore, the psychological impact of conventional weaponry—its familiarity and historical significance—continues to resonate with soldiers and populations alike.

In conclusion, while advancements in military technology have transformed the landscape of warfare, conventional weapons remain vital to modern conflicts. Their accessibility, reliability, versatility, and cultural significance ensure that they will continue to be employed in various forms of combat, making them indispensable tools for state and non-state actors alike. As military strategies evolve, the integration of traditional weaponry with new technologies will likely define future conflicts, ensuring that the legacy of conventional arms endures in the face of innovation.

The Ethics and Legalities of Modern Weapons

The emergence of advanced weapon technologies in recent decades has ignited extensive debates surrounding their ethical implications and legal frameworks. As warfare has evolved, so too have the moral complexities regarding the development, deployment, and regulation of these modern weapons. Key areas of concern include the legality of autonomous weapons systems, the ethical ramifications of drone warfare, and the implications of cyber weapons.

Autonomous Weapons Systems

One of the most significant advancements in modern warfare is the development of autonomous weapons systems, often referred to as "killer robots." These systems possess the capability to select and engage targets without human intervention. Proponents argue that such technologies can reduce human error and save lives by minimizing the need for soldiers on the battlefield. However, critics raise alarming ethical questions about accountability and decision-making. If an autonomous weapon commits a war crime, who is responsible? The manufacturer, the military, or the programmer? The lack of clear accountability raises concerns about the potential for violations of international humanitarian law.

The Campaign to Stop Killer Robots, an international coalition advocating for a preemptive ban on fully autonomous weapons, emphasizes that machines lack the ability to make moral judgments or understand the nuances of human conflict. This argument underscores a fundamental ethical principle: the necessity of human oversight in life-and-death decisions. As discussions continue, calls for a legal framework governing autonomous weapons are increasing, with proposals for international treaties akin to those banning chemical and biological weapons.

Drone Warfare

Drones represent another modern weapon technology that has transformed military operations and sparked ethical debates. While drones offer a tactical advantage by allowing for precise strikes with minimal risk to personnel, their use has raised significant concerns regarding civilian casualties. The U.S. military's drone strikes in countries like Pakistan, Yemen, and Somalia have resulted in numerous unintended civilian deaths, leading to accusations of violating international law.

Critics argue that the remote nature of drone warfare detaches operators from the consequences of their actions, potentially lowering the threshold for the use of lethal force. This shift raises questions about the ethical implications of "targeted killings," particularly when conducted in areas where due process is absent. The lack of transparency surrounding drone operations further complicates the matter, as the public often has limited access to information about the criteria used to designate individuals as targets.

Cyber Weapons

The advent of cyber warfare introduces another dimension to the ethics and legalities of modern weapons. Cyber attacks can disrupt critical infrastructure, cause economic damage, and instill fear without traditional forms of violence. However, the lack of established norms and legal frameworks governing cyber warfare creates a dangerous environment where the potential for escalation is high.

The difficulty in attributing cyber attacks complicates accountability, as state and non-state actors can operate anonymously. This anonymity raises ethical concerns about the potential for indiscriminate harm to civilians and the violation of sovereignty. Moreover, the use of cyber weapons in conflict can blur the lines between combatants and non-combatants, posing challenges for the application of international humanitarian law.

Conclusion

The ethical and legal debates surrounding modern weapon technologies are complex and multifaceted. As advancements continue, the need for robust international dialogue and legal frameworks becomes increasingly urgent. Establishing norms and regulations that address the challenges posed by autonomous weapons, drone warfare, and cyber weapons is critical to ensuring that the evolution of military technology aligns with humanitarian principles and international law. Striking a balance between security and ethical considerations remains essential in shaping the future of warfare and safeguarding human rights in an increasingly complex global landscape.

Chapter 14

Weapons of the 21st Century

The Development of Autonomous Weapons

The evolution of warfare has always been closely intertwined with technological advancement. In the 21st century, one of the most transformative developments in military technology has been the rise of autonomous weapons systems, often referred to as "robots on the battlefield." These systems, powered by artificial intelligence (AI), have the potential to revolutionize combat operations, shifting the nature of warfare and raising significant ethical, legal, and strategic concerns.

Autonomous weapons are defined as systems capable of selecting and engaging targets without human intervention. This technology encompasses a range of platforms, from unmanned aerial vehicles (UAVs) like drones to ground robots and naval vessels that can operate independently. The development of these systems has been driven by several factors, including the need for increased precision in targeting, reduced risk to human soldiers, and the ability to conduct operations in environments that may be hazardous or inaccessible to traditional forces.

One of the primary advantages of autonomous weapons is their potential to enhance operational effectiveness. AI can process vast amounts of data in real time, allowing these systems to make rapid decisions based on battlefield conditions. For instance, drones equipped with sophisticated sensors can identify and track targets with a level of accuracy that minimizes collateral damage. This capability is particularly crucial in urban warfare, where the risk of civilian casualties is high. Furthermore, autonomous systems can operate continuously without the need for rest, enabling sustained surveillance and engagement capabilities.

Despite their advantages, the rise of autonomous weapons raises profound ethical and legal questions. One major concern is the delegation of life-and-death decisions to machines. The lack of human oversight in these systems can lead to unintended consequences, including the potential for malfunction or misidentification of targets. Incidents involving drones that mistakenly strike civilian targets have already raised alarms about accountability and the moral implications of removing human judgment from the decision-making process.

The international community has begun to grapple with these challenges. Discussions at forums such as the United Nations Convention on Certain Conventional Weapons (CCW) have focused on the need for regulations governing the development and use of autonomous weapons. Advocates for a preemptive ban argue that the unpredictability of AI systems poses unacceptable risks, while others contend that such technologies can be developed responsibly with proper oversight.

Additionally, the strategic implications of autonomous weapons are significant. Countries investing in AI and robotics technology may gain a competitive advantage in military operations, potentially leading to an arms race in autonomous weaponry. This scenario raises concerns about destabilization and the erosion of traditional norms of warfare, as nations may be tempted to employ these systems in conflicts where they would not otherwise risk human soldiers.

Moreover, the integration of autonomous weapons into military operations could change the dynamics of warfare itself. The ability to deploy robots on the battlefield may lower the threshold for engaging in conflict, as the perceived risk to human life diminishes. This phenomenon could lead to more frequent military interventions and conflicts, ultimately altering the geopolitical landscape.

In conclusion, the development of autonomous weapons marks a significant milestone in the history of warfare. While these systems offer the potential for enhanced operational efficiency and reduced risks to personnel, they also pose complex ethical, legal, and strategic challenges. As technology continues to advance, the international community faces the urgent task of establishing frameworks that ensure the responsible development and use of autonomous weapons, balancing the interests of national security with the imperative to uphold humanitarian principles and protect human rights. The future of warfare may increasingly hinge on how effectively we navigate these challenges in the age of AI and autonomy.

Directed-Energy Weapons

Directed-energy weapons (DEWs) represent a significant shift in military technology, employing focused energy—such as lasers, microwaves, or particle beams—to incapacitate or destroy targets with precision and speed. These weapons are being developed and deployed across various military applications, promising a new era of warfare characterized by enhanced effectiveness, reduced collateral damage, and lower operational costs.

The Technology Behind Directed-Energy Weapons

At the core of directed-energy weapons is the ability to generate a high concentration of energy in a specific direction. One of the most notable examples is laser weapons, which produce a beam of light that can be focused on a target to cause damage through thermal effects. The basic principle involves the excitation of atoms or molecules to emit photons, which are then amplified and directed. Advanced solid-state lasers, fiber lasers, and chemical lasers are the primary types under development.

Microwave weapons, another category of DEWs, emit bursts of microwave radiation that can disrupt electronic systems or incapacitate personnel without causing permanent injury. These systems can target multiple threats simultaneously, making them especially effective against swarms of drones or incoming missiles.

Particle beam weapons, though still largely experimental, involve accelerating charged or neutral particles to high speeds and directing them at a target. The kinetic energy delivered can potentially cause catastrophic damage, especially to hardened targets.

Advantages of Directed-Energy Weapons

One of the most compelling advantages of DEWs is their cost-effectiveness. Traditional munitions require significant resources in terms of production, storage, and deployment. In contrast, once a directed-energy system is operational, the cost of each shot is significantly lower, often just the cost of electricity. This economic efficiency allows for sustained engagement and defense against multiple threats without depleting ammunition supplies.

Moreover, DEWs offer a high degree of precision. The focused nature of energy beams minimizes collateral damage, a crucial consideration in modern warfare where civilian safety is paramount. This precision makes DEWs particularly appealing for urban combat situations, where distinguishing between combatants and non-combatants can be challenging.

Additionally, the speed of light travel for laser beams means that DEWs can engage targets almost instantaneously, making them effective against fast-moving threats like missiles or drones. This rapid response capability can alter the dynamics of battlefield engagements, providing a significant tactical advantage.

Current Developments and Deployments

As of 2023, various military organizations worldwide are actively researching and deploying DEWs. The U.S. military, for instance, has tested systems like the Laser Weapon System (LaWS) and the High Energy Laser with Integrated Optical-dazzler and Surveillance (HELIOS) on naval vessels. These systems have demonstrated the ability to disable drones and small boats, showcasing their operational viability.

Internationally, countries like China and Russia are also investing heavily in DEW technologies, reflecting a global race to develop effective directed-energy capabilities. The potential for DEWs to redefine air and missile defense systems is a significant focus, with the ability to neutralize threats before they reach their intended targets.

Challenges and Future Outlook

Despite their promise, directed-energy weapons face challenges, including atmospheric interference, heat dissipation, and the need for robust power sources. For instance, weather conditions, such as rain or fog, can scatter laser beams, reducing effectiveness. Ongoing research aims to overcome these limitations, focusing on improving power efficiency and developing systems that can operate effectively in diverse environmental conditions.

As technology advances, directed-energy weapons are expected to play an increasingly prominent role in military arsenals. Their integration into existing systems, combined with advancements in artificial intelligence and machine learning for target acquisition and tracking, could further enhance their operational effectiveness.

In conclusion, directed-energy weapons represent a paradigm shift in military technology, offering new capabilities that promise to change the landscape of warfare. As development continues and challenges are addressed, DEWs are likely to become a staple in modern military operations, reshaping strategies and engagements in the years to come.

Hypersonic Weapons

The advancement of hypersonic weapons represents one of the most significant developments in military technology, marking a pivotal shift in the capabilities of modern warfare. Hypersonic weapons, defined as those that travel at speeds exceeding Mach 5 (five times the speed of sound), are designed to maneuver in the atmosphere at such high velocities that they can evade traditional missile defense systems. This capability creates a new arms race, as nations strive to develop and deploy these advanced technologies to gain a strategic advantage.

Development of Hypersonic Technology

The development of hypersonic weapons is rooted in research and innovation in aerospace technology, materials science, and propulsion systems. Countries such as the United States, Russia, and China have invested heavily in this area, driven by the need to maintain national security and military superiority. Hypersonic weapons typically fall into two categories: hypersonic glide vehicles (HGVs) and hypersonic cruise missiles (HCMs).

- Hypersonic Glide Vehicles: These weapons are launched using conventional rockets and then glide towards their targets at hypersonic speeds, taking advantage of their ability to maneuver unpredictably. This unpredictability complicates detection and interception, significantly enhancing their effectiveness.

- Hypersonic Cruise Missiles: These missiles utilize advanced air-breathing engines to maintain hypersonic speeds throughout their flight. They can operate at lower altitudes and have the ability to alter their trajectory mid-flight, making them difficult to anticipate and counter.

The race to develop hypersonic capabilities has intensified, with countries testing various prototypes and conducting research to refine their technologies. The urgency to advance in this area stems from the recognition that hypersonic weapons could fundamentally alter military strategy and global power dynamics.

Implications for Global Security

The introduction of hypersonic weapons into military arsenals raises significant implications for global security and strategic stability. The key concerns include:

1. Erosion of Deterrence: Traditional deterrence strategies, which rely on the threat of retaliation, may be undermined by the speed and maneuverability of hypersonic weapons. Their ability to reach targets quickly and without warning can create a situation where adversaries feel pressured to act preemptively, increasing the risk of conflict.

2. Challenges to Missile Defense: Current missile defense systems are primarily designed to intercept ballistic missiles, which follow predictable trajectories. The erratic flight paths and extreme speeds of hypersonic weapons pose a substantial challenge to existing defense protocols, necessitating the development of new systems to counter these threats.

3. Escalation of Arms Race: The pursuit of hypersonic technology has the potential to trigger an arms race among nuclear and conventional powers. Nations may feel compelled to develop their hypersonic capabilities or enhance their existing arsenals to deter potential adversaries, leading to an increase in global military spending and tensions.

4. International Treaties and Agreements: The development of hypersonic weapons complicates existing arms control frameworks. The introduction of such technologies may prompt nations to reconsider treaties like the Intermediate-Range Nuclear Forces Treaty (INF), which previously aimed to limit the proliferation of certain classes of missiles. New agreements may be necessary to address the challenges posed by hypersonic weaponry.

Conclusion

As hypersonic technology continues to evolve, it poses complex challenges and opportunities for global security. The race to develop and deploy these weapons not only alters the landscape of military strategy but also necessitates a reevaluation of existing deterrence doctrines and arms control agreements. Nations must navigate the delicate balance of maintaining security while preventing escalation into a new arms race, emphasizing the need for dialogue and international cooperation in addressing the implications of hypersonic weaponry. The future of warfare may hinge significantly on how these developments are managed on the global stage.

Space as the Next Battlefield

The advent of modern technology has ushered in a new frontier in warfare: outer space. Over the past few decades, nations have increasingly recognized space not only as a domain for exploration but also as a strategic arena that can influence terrestrial conflicts. The potential for conflict in space has prompted military leaders and policymakers to consider weaponizing this vast expanse, raising complex questions about security, ethics, and the future of international relations.

The Strategic Importance of Space

Space has become integral to national security. Satellites are crucial for communication, navigation, reconnaissance, and surveillance. The loss of these assets could severely cripple a nation's ability to conduct military operations on Earth. As a result, the protection of space assets has become paramount. Moreover, the increasing reliance on space for civilian applications, such as global positioning systems (GPS) and telecommunications, underscores its importance as a strategic resource.

Given these stakes, the idea of weaponizing space—developing and deploying weapons systems that can operate beyond the Earth's atmosphere—has emerged as a significant concern. Countries like the United States, Russia, and China are investing in technologies that could enable them to gain a military advantage in space. This includes the development of anti-satellite (ASAT) weapons, which are designed to disable or destroy enemy satellites, thereby rendering them vulnerable in a conflict scenario.

Types of Space-Based Weapons

The concept of space-based weapons encompasses various systems, including kinetic and non-kinetic options. Kinetic weapons involve physical projectiles or missiles designed to collide with or destroy targets in space. For instance, the U.S. and Russia have conducted tests of ASAT weapons capable of targeting satellites in low Earth orbit.

On the other hand, non-kinetic weapons may utilize directed energy, such as lasers or electromagnetic pulse (EMP) weapons, to disrupt or damage satellite operations without physical collision. Such technologies could incapacitate electronic systems, creating a significant tactical advantage while minimizing the risk of space debris.

The Risks and Challenges of Space Warfare

The weaponization of space presents numerous risks. First, the creation of space-based weapons could lead to an arms race, as nations strive to develop advanced technologies to counteract potential threats. This could escalate tensions and increase the likelihood of military conflict, not only in space but also on Earth.

Additionally, the proliferation of space debris is a critical concern. Collisions between weapons and operational satellites could generate debris that endangers other spacecraft and satellites, potentially leading to a cascading effect known as the Kessler Syndrome. This phenomenon could cripple vital space infrastructure and adversely impact both military and civilian operations.

International Law and Governance

The legal framework governing the use of space is currently limited. The 1967 Outer Space Treaty, which forms the basis of international space law, emphasizes that space should be used for peaceful purposes. However, the treaty does not explicitly prohibit the development of space-based weapons. As nations continue to explore military options in space, there is an urgent need for new agreements and regulations to govern the use of space and prevent an arms race.

Conclusion

The prospect of weaponizing space poses significant challenges for global security and international relations. As nations increasingly view space as a critical domain for military operations, the need for cooperative international governance becomes ever more pressing. Balancing national security interests with the imperative to maintain peace in outer space will require diplomatic efforts, transparency, and a commitment to preventing the militarization of what should remain a domain for exploration and cooperation. The future of warfare may well depend on how the international community navigates these complex issues in the coming years.

The Future of Military Technology

As we stand on the precipice of significant technological advancements, the future of military technology is poised for groundbreaking innovation that will reshape the landscape of warfare. Emerging technologies, including artificial intelligence (AI), robotics, and advanced materials, promise to revolutionize how military operations are conducted. This section speculates on these advancements and their potential implications for global security, military strategy, and society.

1. Artificial Intelligence and Autonomous Systems

AI is increasingly being integrated into military applications, enhancing decision-making processes and operational efficiency. Future military systems are likely to leverage AI for data analysis, threat detection, and automated responses. Autonomous drones and unmanned ground vehicles could conduct surveillance, reconnaissance, and even engage in combat without direct human oversight. While these advancements offer strategic advantages, they also raise ethical concerns over accountability in warfare and the potential for unintended escalation. The concept of "killer robots," autonomous systems capable of making lethal decisions, presents a challenge for international law and ethical frameworks governing warfare.

2. Directed-Energy Weapons

Directed-energy weapons (DEWs), which utilize focused energy such as lasers and microwave beams to disable or destroy targets, are gaining traction in military applications. The advantages of DEWs include precision targeting, reduced ammunition costs, and the ability to counter aerial threats like drones and missiles. As this technology matures, it could lead to a paradigm shift in air defense strategies, enabling militaries to intercept incoming threats with unprecedented accuracy. Additionally, the potential for DEWs to be deployed in a non-lethal capacity for crowd control raises questions about their use in domestic scenarios.

3. Hypersonic Weapons

Hypersonic weapons, capable of traveling at speeds exceeding Mach 5, represent a new arms race in military technology. Their speed and maneuverability make them difficult to detect and intercept, posing a significant challenge to existing defense systems. As nations invest in hypersonic capabilities, the balance of power could shift dramatically, necessitating the development of advanced countermeasures. The strategic implications of hypersonic technology extend to deterrence theories, as countries with such capabilities may alter their approach to conflict and diplomacy.

4. Cyber Warfare and Information Operations

As warfare increasingly becomes a contest of information and data, the realm of cyber warfare will expand. Nations are investing in capabilities to disrupt adversaries' critical infrastructure and to conduct espionage via cyberspace. The future will likely see a greater emphasis on cyber defense strategies and the establishment of norms governing state behavior in cyberspace. The potential for cyberattacks to escalate into kinetic conflict poses a significant risk, necessitating robust international agreements to mitigate the consequences of digital warfare.

5. Biotechnology and Human Enhancement

The intersection of biotechnology and military applications could lead to enhanced soldier capabilities, including improved physical performance and resilience to injury. Genetic engineering and advanced medical technologies may create soldiers who can endure harsher conditions and recover from injuries more effectively. However, these advancements raise ethical questions about consent, the definition of a soldier, and the long-term societal impacts of human enhancement.

6. Space as a New Frontier

The militarization of space is becoming a critical aspect of national security strategies. As countries develop anti-satellite weapons and deploy military assets in orbit, the potential for conflicts in space will grow. The implications of space warfare could extend to civilian infrastructure, as satellite systems are integral to global communication, navigation, and weather forecasting. An arms race in space technology could complicate international relations and require new frameworks for governance.

Conclusion

The future of military technology is characterized by rapid advancement and complex challenges. As nations harness emerging technologies, the implications for warfare, international security, and ethical considerations will be profound. Preparing for these changes requires proactive engagement in international dialogue, regulation, and ethical deliberation to ensure that advancements in military technology promote security while minimizing the risks of conflict and escalation. The balance between innovation and ethical responsibility will be critical in shaping the future of warfare and global stability.

Chapter 15

The Impact of Weapons on Society

Weapons and Social Hierarchy

Throughout history, weapons have played a crucial role in shaping social structures and hierarchies, influencing who wields power and how that power is maintained or challenged. The relationship between weaponry and social organization is deeply intertwined, reflecting broader themes of control, dominance, resistance, and the dynamics of power.

In early human societies, the development and use of weapons were closely linked to survival and the establishment of social order. For instance, the advancement from rudimentary stone tools to more sophisticated weapons like spears and bows significantly enhanced hunting capabilities, contributing to food security. This food security, in turn, allowed for the establishment of more complex social structures, as surplus resources facilitated population growth and the rise of distinct social roles. Those who possessed superior weapons often found themselves in positions of leadership, as the ability to protect and provide became synonymous with authority.

As civilizations evolved, so did the sophistication of weaponry and its implications for social hierarchy. The emergence of bronze weapons marked a significant turning point, where access to advanced metallurgy became a critical factor in determining social status. Societies that could produce and control these weapons often dominated their neighbors, both militarily and economically. This created a clear demarcation between classes, where warrior elites—often the ruling class—held significant power, while lower classes were relegated to subordinate roles. The symbolism of weapons, such as swords and armor, further solidified this hierarchy, as they became emblems of authority and social status.

The development of feudal systems during the Middle Ages exemplifies the relationship between weapons and social hierarchy. Knights, who were heavily armed and armored, occupied a privileged position within the feudal structure. Their ability to control land and resources was directly linked to their military prowess, facilitated by their access to advanced weaponry such as the longbow, crossbow, and later, gunpowder-based arms. The social order was thus maintained through a combination of military might and loyalty, with weapons serving as a means of both defense and oppression.

In more modern contexts, the industrial revolution further transformed the relationship between weapons and social dynamics. The mass production of firearms and artillery led to the democratization of military power, as states could equip larger armies and civilians gained easier access to weaponry. This shift posed challenges to existing power structures, as revolutions and uprisings became more feasible. The American and French Revolutions, for example, were fueled by the desire for equality and justice against oppressive regimes, underscoring the role of weapons in challenging social hierarchies.

However, the proliferation of weapons also fostered new forms of control. The rise of the state and the establishment of laws governing weapon ownership created a complex dynamic where those in power regulated the very means of resistance. The relationship between weaponry and social order can thus be seen as a double-edged sword: while weapons can empower marginalized groups, they can also be wielded by those in authority to suppress dissent.

In contemporary society, the impact of weapons on social hierarchy persists. The global arms trade, military interventions, and the availability of small arms have significant implications for social structures worldwide. In many regions, access to weapons continues to determine power dynamics, influencing everything from local governance to international relations.

In conclusion, the influence of weapons on social hierarchies is a profound and multifaceted aspect of human history. Weapons have not only shaped the means of conflict but have also defined the contours of power, authority, and resistance. Understanding this relationship is crucial for comprehending the ongoing challenges of social equity and justice in a world still grappling with the consequences of armed conflict and the pervasive influence of weaponry.

Weapons and Law

The regulation of weapons and arms ownership has evolved significantly over centuries, reflecting societal values, technological advancements, and the changing dynamics of warfare and security. This evolution can be traced from ancient times through to the modern legal frameworks that govern arms control today.

In ancient societies, the regulation of arms was often rudimentary, with local customs and tribal laws dictating the ownership and use of weapons. The primary focus was on maintaining order and ensuring that individuals could protect themselves and their communities. As civilizations advanced, so too did the need for more structured approaches to weapon regulation. The establishment of kingdoms and empires led to formalized laws, such as those seen in Roman law, which included regulations concerning the manufacture, ownership, and use of weapons, often linked to social status and military service.

The Middle Ages introduced further complexity to arms regulation with the feudal system, where lords controlled the distribution of arms among their vassals. This period saw the emergence of the concept of "just war," which intertwined ethical considerations with the use of force, laying the groundwork for later legal frameworks. The rise of nation-states in the early modern period further necessitated comprehensive arms regulations, particularly as gunpowder weapons transformed warfare. States began to implement laws governing the manufacture and ownership of firearms, recognizing the need to prevent uprisings and maintain public order.

The 19th century marked a significant turning point in the regulation of arms, fueled by the industrial revolution and the proliferation of new weapon technologies. Countries began to establish formal arms control measures, often in response to the devastating effects of warfare. The Hague Conventions of 1899 and 1907 represented early attempts to codify international law regarding the conduct of war and the treatment of combatants and non-combatants, indirectly influencing arms regulation by establishing norms around the types of weapons permissible in conflict.

The aftermath of World War I and the subsequent rise of totalitarian regimes highlighted the need for more stringent arms regulations to prevent the escalation of violence. The League of Nations sought to address these concerns with various disarmament initiatives, although these efforts faced challenges due to geopolitical tensions and the inability of member states to reach consensus.

Following World War II, the establishment of the United Nations (UN) and its various arms control treaties marked a new era in the regulation of weapons. The UN Charter emphasized the importance of collective security and the need for disarmament as a means to prevent future conflicts. Notable treaties, such as the Treaty on the Non-Proliferation of Nuclear Weapons (NPT) in 1968, sought to curb the spread of nuclear weapons and promote disarmament among nuclear-armed states.

In more recent decades, the global arms trade has come under scrutiny, leading to the development of international agreements aimed at regulating the trade of conventional arms. The Arms Trade Treaty (ATT), adopted in 2013, represents a significant step towards establishing a framework for the responsible trade of arms, aiming to prevent human rights abuses and promote international peace and security.

The evolution of arms regulation continues to respond to new challenges, including the rise of non-state actors, the proliferation of small arms, and advancements in technology. Legal frameworks now address issues such as cyber warfare and the use of drones, reflecting the changing nature of conflict and security concerns in the 21st century.

In conclusion, the regulation of arms has evolved from informal customs to comprehensive legal frameworks, shaped by historical events, technological advancements, and the ongoing quest for global peace and security. As societies continue to grapple with the implications of weapon ownership and use, the evolution of laws governing arms remains a critical component of contemporary discussions on security, human rights, and international relations.

The Role of Weapons in Revolutions and Resistance

Throughout history, weapons have served as critical instruments in the struggle for freedom, autonomy, and social change. From the earliest instances of rebellion against oppressive regimes to contemporary movements for justice, weapons have played an essential role in shaping the dynamics of revolutions and resistance movements. This section explores how weapons have been utilized as tools of empowerment, both enabling and complicating the quest for social and political transformation.

Historical Context

The relationship between weaponry and revolutionary movements can be traced back to ancient societies. For instance, the use of spears and bows by early humans not only facilitated hunting but also provided means for self-defense and rebellion against tyrannical groups. Fast forward to the late medieval period, the use of longbows by English forces during the Hundred Years' War exemplified the impact of accessible weaponry in leveling the playing field against more established powers. The longbowmen's success demonstrated how common people could wield weapons to challenge feudal lords and establish a sense of agency.

The American Revolution

The American Revolution (1775–1783) serves as a pivotal example of the role of weapons in revolt against colonial oppression. The colonists, feeling the weight of British tyranny and taxation, armed themselves with firearms and formed militias. The famous phrase "the right to bear arms" emerged from this context, emphasizing the belief that an armed populace is necessary for the defense of liberty. The battles of Lexington and Concord saw the first shots fired, symbolizing the power of armed resistance against a dominant empire. Weapons were not merely tools of war; they became symbols of freedom and resistance, galvanizing public support and attracting international allies.

The French Revolution

Similarly, the French Revolution (1789–1799) illustrated how weapons could transform societal structures. The storming of the Bastille, a fortress prison, was not only a significant tactical victory for the revolutionaries but also a powerful symbol of the uprising against oppression. The revolution saw the proliferation of weapons among the populace, with the guillotine becoming an emblem of both revolutionary justice and terror. The accessibility of firearms and the establishment of revolutionary armies allowed citizens to partake in the struggle for equality and rights, fundamentally altering the political landscape of France and inspiring subsequent revolutions worldwide.

Modern Resistance Movements

In the 20th and 21st centuries, the role of weapons in resistance movements evolved alongside technological advancements. Armed groups such as the Viet Cong during the Vietnam War employed guerrilla tactics, utilizing small arms and improvised explosive devices to counter a technologically superior opponent. Their success highlighted how even limited resources could lead to significant military victories through strategic use of weapons and local knowledge of terrain.

Moreover, contemporary movements, such as those in Syria and Libya during the Arab Spring, have illustrated the dual-edged nature of weaponry. While weapons empower rebels and provide a means for uprising, they can also result in chaos, exacerbate violence, and lead to humanitarian crises. The proliferation of firearms in these contexts raises ethical questions about the consequences of armed resistance and the potential for weapons to undermine the very goals of liberation.

Conclusion

In conclusion, weapons have long played a complex role in revolutions and resistance movements, serving as both instruments of empowerment and sources of conflict. They have allowed oppressed populations to challenge authority and assert their rights, but they also bring the risk of violence and societal fragmentation. As history shows, while weapons can facilitate change, their presence often complicates the path to a just and stable society. The legacy of weapons in revolutions serves as a reminder of the ongoing struggle for freedom and the ethical considerations that accompany the fight against oppression.

The Ethics of Weapon Development and Use

The development and use of weapons have long been at the center of ethical debates, raising complex moral questions about their creation, deployment, and the consequences of their use. As technology advances, these debates become increasingly pertinent, especially with the emergence of new weaponry such as autonomous systems, drones, and cyber weapons. The ethical considerations surrounding weaponry can be divided into several key areas: the justification for the use of force, the impact on civilians, the responsibility of developers and users, and the implications of emerging technologies.

Justification for the Use of Force

At the core of the ethical debate surrounding weaponry is the question of when, if ever, the use of force is justified. Just war theory, a doctrine that dates back to antiquity, provides a framework for evaluating the moral legitimacy of warfare. According to this theory, a war can only be just if it meets certain criteria, including just cause, proportionality, and discrimination between combatants and non-combatants. However, the application of these principles is often contested. For instance, the notion of preemptive strikes raises ethical concerns about the justification of an attack based on perceived threats versus actual aggression. This ambiguity can lead to conflicts where the lines between justified and unjustified violence are blurred.

Impact on Civilians

The ethical implications of weapons extend beyond the battlefield into civilian life. The principle of proportionality requires that the anticipated military advantage from an attack must outweigh the potential harm to civilians and civilian infrastructure. This principle becomes increasingly problematic in modern warfare, particularly with the advent of high-tech weaponry and military strategies that may unintentionally result in significant civilian casualties. The use of drones, for example, while touted for their precision, has raised serious ethical questions regarding "collateral damage." The psychological impact on civilian populations in conflict zones, coupled with the often indiscriminate nature of certain weapons, necessitates a reevaluation of ethical frameworks governing their use.

Responsibility of Developers and Users

Another critical aspect of the ethical discourse on weaponry concerns the responsibilities of those who develop, manufacture, and deploy weapons. Engineers, scientists, and military personnel may grapple with complex moral dilemmas about the technologies they create or use. The ethical implications of creating autonomous weapons systems, which can make decisions without human intervention, raise questions about accountability. Who is responsible if such a weapon causes unintended harm? The lack of clear accountability could lead to increased risks and a potential erosion of ethical standards in military operations.

Emerging Technologies and Future Considerations

As weapon technology continues to evolve, new ethical challenges arise. The development of artificial intelligence (AI) in military applications poses significant concerns regarding the potential for autonomous weapons to operate independently of human oversight. The possibility of such weapons making life-and-death decisions raises profound ethical dilemmas. Furthermore, cyber warfare introduces complexities regarding the traditional rules of engagement, as the digital landscape lacks the clear boundaries of physical warfare.

In conclusion, the ethics of weapon development and use is a multifaceted issue that requires ongoing examination and discourse. As societies confront the moral implications of advanced weaponry, it is essential to engage in critical discussions that balance national security needs with humanitarian concerns. Developing robust ethical frameworks that prioritize the minimization of harm, accountability, and the well-being of civilians is vital in navigating the complexities of modern warfare. The future of weaponry will undoubtedly challenge our moral compass, demanding a thoughtful and principled approach to its evolution and deployment.

Weapons in Popular Culture

The portrayal of weapons in popular culture—spanning literature, film, video games, and other media—has profoundly influenced public perception and societal attitudes toward violence, conflict, and the nature of weaponry itself. This representation often blurs the lines between myth and reality, shaping both the understanding and the expectations surrounding weapons and warfare.

The Glamourization of Weapons

One of the most significant effects of media representation is the glamorization of weapons and their use. Action movies often depict firearms as sleek, powerful tools wielded by heroic protagonists, creating an allure around firearms that can overshadow their destructive capabilities. Characters wielding weapons with precision and ease can lead audiences to perceive firearms as instruments of empowerment rather than tools of violence, reinforcing the idea that weapons confer status and capability.

This portrayal can be particularly problematic, as it often overlooks the real-life consequences of gun violence. For example, movies like "John Wick" or the "Die Hard" series present gunfights as choreographed, almost balletic encounters, where protagonists emerge unscathed despite the chaos around them. Such depictions can desensitize viewers to the brutality of actual gunfights, where the reality is far more grim and chaotic.

The Role of Video Games

Video games, too, play a pivotal role in shaping perceptions of weapons. Titles like "Call of Duty" and "Counter-Strike" immerse players in virtual combat scenarios where weapons are central to gameplay. While these games often include educational elements, such as strategic thinking and teamwork, they can also normalize violence and weapon use. The interactive nature of these games can lead to a disassociation between the virtual consequences of weapon use and their real-world implications.

Moreover, the graphic nature of video games can create a false sense of familiarity with weapons. Many players may develop an understanding of firearms and military tactics through gaming, which can misconstrue the complexities and ethical considerations surrounding real-life warfare and armaments. This detachment can lead to a perception among younger audiences that weapons are integral to identity and social status, influencing their behavior and attitudes toward violence.

Myths Versus Reality

The myths surrounding weapons in popular culture often extend to misconceptions about their functionality and effectiveness. Films and television frequently exaggerate the capabilities of weapons, portraying them as infallible and always lethal. In reality, many factors determine the efficacy of a weapon, including the skill of the user, environmental conditions, and mechanical reliability. Such oversimplifications can contribute to a misunderstanding of how guns and other weapons operate in real life.

Additionally, the romanticized portrayal of historical warfare—seen in movies like "Gladiator" or "300"—can create an inaccurate narrative about the nature of combat and the experience of soldiers. These portrayals often omit the gruesome realities of war, including the psychological toll it takes on individuals, the chaos of battle, and the socio-political contexts in which these conflicts arise.

Influencing Public Perception

The cumulative impact of these media representations is significant. They can shape public perception about the necessity of weapons for personal security, influence legislative debates on gun control, and affect societal attitudes toward military engagement. As audiences internalize these portrayals, they may develop a skewed understanding of the role weapons play in society, often viewing them through a lens of empowerment rather than one of fear and destruction.

In conclusion, the portrayal of weapons in popular culture serves as a double-edged sword. While it can engage audiences and stimulate discussions about conflict and security, it also risks perpetuating myths that obscure the harsh realities of violence. As consumers of media, it is essential to approach these representations critically, recognizing the difference between the dramatized narratives presented on screen and the complex, often painful realities of weapon use in the world.

Chapter 16

The Global Arms Trade

The Economics of Weaponry

The arms trade represents a complex and multifaceted sector of the global economy, driven by intricate dynamics of supply and demand. Understanding how this trade operates requires an examination of both the economic principles that underpin it and the geopolitical factors that influence its flow.

At its core, the arms trade operates on basic economic principles of supply and demand, where the demand for military capabilities influences production, distribution, and pricing of weapons. The demand for armaments can arise from a variety of sources, including national defense needs, geopolitical tensions, and domestic security concerns. Governments often allocate substantial portions of their budgets to defense spending, which creates a consistent demand for military equipment ranging from small arms to advanced missile systems.

On the supply side, the arms industry comprises a network of manufacturers, suppliers, and intermediaries that produce and distribute weaponry. Major arms-producing countries, such as the United States, Russia, China, and several European nations, have established robust defense industries capable of producing a wide array of military hardware. These countries not only meet their own defense requirements but also engage in international arms sales, supplying weapons to allied nations and, at times, to conflict zones.

The dynamics of demand in the arms trade are significantly influenced by geopolitical factors. For instance, countries in conflict-prone regions or those with ongoing territorial disputes often ramp up their military capabilities, leading to increased demand for arms. Furthermore, emerging threats, such as terrorism and cyber warfare, compel nations to invest in new technologies and capabilities, further driving demand.

Economic implications of the arms trade extend beyond mere supply and demand. The trade influences national economies, creating jobs, fostering technological innovation, and contributing to GDP. In many countries, the defense industry is a significant employer, providing skilled jobs and stimulating local economies. Moreover, arms exports can enhance a country's economic standing and geopolitical influence, allowing nations to forge alliances and exert power through military cooperation.

However, the arms trade also presents challenges and ethical dilemmas. The proliferation of weapons can exacerbate conflicts, contribute to human rights abuses, and destabilize regions. The flow of arms into conflict zones often prolongs wars and increases civilian casualties, raising moral questions about the responsibilities of arms producers and exporters.

In response to these challenges, international regulations and agreements have been established, such as the Arms Trade Treaty (ATT), which aims to promote responsible arms transfers and prevent the illicit trade of weapons. These frameworks seek to create a balance between the economic benefits of arms sales and the need for global security and human rights protections.

Furthermore, the illegal arms trade poses a significant challenge to the regulated arms market. Black markets thrive in regions where legal arms flows are restricted or where political instability prevails. This illicit trade complicates the efforts to regulate the arms industry, as it undermines legal frameworks and facilitates the proliferation of arms to non-state actors and terrorist organizations.

In conclusion, the economics of weaponry, driven by the principles of supply and demand, plays a crucial role in shaping global security dynamics. While the arms trade can stimulate economies and foster innovation, it also raises serious ethical concerns and implications for human rights. As the global landscape continues to evolve, the balance between the economic benefits of arms trade and the need for responsible regulation remains a critical challenge for policymakers and society as a whole. Addressing these complexities requires a nuanced understanding of both the economic motivations behind arms trade and the broader impact on global peace and stability.

The Role of Governments in the Arms Trade

The global arms trade is a complex system that significantly affects international relations, security dynamics, and the socio-political landscape of nations. Governments play a crucial role in shaping, regulating, and influencing this market, leveraging arms trade to fulfill national interests, project power, and maintain strategic alliances. This section delves into the multifaceted ways in which states govern the arms trade, including regulatory frameworks, economic influences, and geopolitical considerations.

Regulatory Frameworks

Governments establish regulatory frameworks that dictate the terms of arms production, sale, and distribution both domestically and internationally. These regulations are often structured around national security concerns, foreign policy objectives, and compliance with international treaties. The Arms Trade Treaty (ATT), adopted in 2013, exemplifies a global effort to regulate the arms trade by establishing common standards for the transfer of conventional weapons. Governments that ratify the ATT commit to assessing the risk of weapons being used to violate human rights or international humanitarian law before approving arms exports.

In addition to international treaties, domestic laws also play a significant role. These laws can establish licensing requirements for arms manufacturers, export controls that require government approval for the sale of weapons abroad, and regulations that prevent the proliferation of arms to non-state actors or nations under embargoes. Governments, therefore, maintain a gatekeeping role that dictates the flow of arms globally.

Economic Influence

The arms trade is not just a matter of security; it is also a substantial economic enterprise. Governments influence the global arms market through procurement policies, defense spending allocations, and support for domestic arms manufacturers. By prioritizing military contracts, states can stimulate their economies, create jobs, and foster technological advancements. This economic incentive often leads to a symbiotic relationship between governments and defense contractors, where military expenditure becomes a critical driver of national economic policy.

Furthermore, state-led initiatives can enhance the competitiveness of domestic arms producers in the international market. This includes export financing, subsidies for research and development, and participation in multinational defense projects. Governments may also engage in strategic partnerships with other nations to co-develop military technologies, thereby reinforcing their influence in the global arms market.

Geopolitical Considerations

The arms trade is deeply intertwined with geopolitical strategies. Governments often engage in arms sales as a means to solidify alliances, exert influence over client states, and counterbalance adversaries. For instance, the United States has historically leveraged arms sales as a means to strengthen partnerships in regions of strategic importance, such as the Middle East and Asia. By providing advanced weaponry to allied nations, the U.S. not only enhances their military capabilities but also reinforces its own geopolitical interests.

Moreover, arms sales can serve as a tool of diplomacy. Nations may use arms trade negotiations to facilitate broader diplomatic agreements or to secure cooperation on issues ranging from trade to environmental policy. In some cases, arms sales are tied to political conditions, where recipient countries must adhere to certain human rights standards or strategic commitments in exchange for military support.

Conclusion

In summary, governments wield significant influence over the global arms trade through regulatory frameworks, economic policies, and geopolitical strategies. The interplay of these factors shapes the dynamics of the arms market and reflects broader national interests. As the international security landscape continues to evolve, the role of governments in the arms trade will remain a critical area of focus for policymakers and scholars alike, demanding ongoing scrutiny to balance the imperatives of national security with global peace and stability. The challenge lies in ensuring that arms trade practices contribute positively to international relations and do not exacerbate conflicts or human rights abuses.

The Impact of the Arms Trade on Global Conflicts

The global arms trade is a significant factor in shaping international relations and conflicts. It involves the legal and illegal transfer of weapons and military technology across borders, influencing the dynamics of power and stability within nations and regions. The availability of weapons has profound effects on international stability, conflict escalation, and the nature of warfare itself.

The Proliferation of Arms and Conflict Dynamics

The proliferation of weapons has a direct correlation with the outbreak and duration of conflicts. When weapons are readily available, it often emboldens groups—be they state actors or non-state insurgents—to engage in armed confrontations. For instance, the widespread distribution of small arms in conflict zones, such as in Africa and the Middle East, has led to protracted violence and instability. The availability of arms can escalate minor disputes into full-fledged wars, as seen in the Rwandan Genocide and the ongoing civil strife in Syria.

Moreover, the arms trade can exacerbate existing tensions between nations. For example, countries engaged in territorial disputes may increase their military capabilities through imports, leading to an arms race that heightens the likelihood of conflict. In such scenarios, the availability of advanced weaponry can shift the balance of power, encouraging aggressive posturing and militarization.

Economic Incentives and Conflict Resolution

The arms trade is also driven by economic incentives, often prioritizing profit over peace. Arms manufacturers and exporting nations may have vested interests in sustaining conflicts, as ongoing warfare can lead to lucrative contracts. This dynamic complicates conflict resolution efforts, as external parties may be unwilling to support peace initiatives that threaten their economic interests. Additionally, countries that rely on arms exports for economic growth may resist disarmament or arms control agreements, further entrenching conflict cycles.

Humanitarian Consequences and Civilian Impact

The impact of the arms trade goes beyond geopolitical dynamics; it has severe humanitarian consequences. The influx of weapons into conflict zones often results in increased civilian casualties and suffering. In many instances, the most affected populations are those already vulnerable due to socioeconomic instability. The availability of arms can lead to widespread human rights abuses, as armed groups may target civilians, engage in massacres, or utilize sexual violence as a weapon of war. The International Committee of the Red Cross has documented numerous instances where the arms trade has contributed to violations of international humanitarian law.

The Role of International Regulation

Recognizing the detrimental effects of the arms trade on global stability, international efforts have been made to regulate and control the trade in weapons. Treaties such as the Arms Trade Treaty (ATT) aim to establish global standards for arms transfers, ensuring they do not exacerbate conflicts or contribute to human rights violations. However, enforcement remains a challenge, particularly in regions where governance is weak, and illicit trafficking flourishes.

Conclusion: A Complex Relationship

In conclusion, the impact of the arms trade on global conflicts is multifaceted. While the availability of weapons can empower nations and groups, it also poses significant risks to international stability and humanitarian welfare. The proliferation of arms can escalate conflicts, empower aggressors, and lead to severe human rights violations. As the global community grapples with these challenges, a concerted effort towards better regulation, transparency, and accountability in the arms trade is vital. By addressing the root causes of conflict and promoting disarmament, nations can work towards a more peaceful global landscape, where the availability of weapons does not dictate the trajectory of human affairs.

The Illegal Arms Trade

The illegal arms trade represents a significant challenge to global security, exacerbating conflicts, undermining governments, and fueling violence. This clandestine market operates outside the bounds of international law, facilitating the proliferation of weapons to non-state actors, criminal organizations, and oppressive regimes. Understanding the dynamics of the illegal arms trade requires an examination of the methods of smuggling, the actors involved, and the broader implications for society.

Nature and Scope of the Illegal Arms Trade

The illegal arms trade encompasses the transfer of weapons and ammunition that contravenes national and international laws. It includes a wide range of weaponry—from small arms and light weapons (SALW) to more sophisticated military equipment. Estimates suggest that the illicit arms trade generates billions of dollars annually, with the United Nations and various NGOs highlighting the trade's role in perpetuating violence and destabilization in conflict regions.

Key actors in this trade include arms dealers, organized crime syndicates, and corrupt officials who exploit loopholes in legal frameworks. These individuals and groups often operate on a global scale, leveraging international connections to source weapons from countries with lax export controls. For instance, former Soviet states have been identified as significant suppliers of illicit arms, due to their surplus military stockpiles and the existence of corruption within governmental ranks.

Mechanisms of Smuggling

Smuggling techniques used in the illegal arms trade are diverse and often sophisticated. Traffickers utilize established networks and routes to evade detection, frequently operating in chaos-ridden regions where law enforcement is weak or non-existent. Common methods of smuggling include:

1. Concealment: Arms traffickers often hide weapons within legitimate cargo shipments, disguising them among everyday goods. This method can involve false documentation to mislead customs officials about the nature and destination of the cargo.

2. Corruption: Bribery plays a crucial role in facilitating arms smuggling. Corrupt officials may turn a blind eye to suspicious shipments or actively assist traffickers in exchange for financial gain. This corruption undermines governance and contributes to the cycle of violence in affected regions.

3. Transshipment: Arms are frequently shipped through third-party countries before reaching their final destination. This practice complicates tracking and accountability, as weapons can change hands multiple times, making it difficult for authorities to trace their origins.

4. Use of Technology: The rise of digital communication and encryption technologies has enabled traffickers to coordinate operations more securely. Dark web marketplaces facilitate the exchange of weapons, further obscuring the identities of buyers and sellers.

Implications of the Illegal Arms Trade

The consequences of the illegal arms trade are profound and multifaceted. In war-torn regions, the influx of illicit weapons exacerbates violence, prolonging conflicts and leading to increased civilian casualties. For instance, in areas like the Middle East and sub-Saharan Africa, armed groups can gain access to advanced weaponry, challenging state authorities and destabilizing entire nations.

Moreover, the illegal arms trade undermines international efforts to regulate arms proliferation. It complicates disarmament initiatives and hampers peacekeeping efforts, as peacekeepers often face heavily armed factions that possess weapons acquired through illicit means. This dynamic can lead to cycles of violence that are difficult to break.

Conclusion

Tackling the illegal arms trade requires a multifaceted approach, including enhanced international cooperation, stricter regulations, and increased transparency in arms transfers. The challenge lies not only in the enforcement of existing laws but also in addressing the root causes of demand for illicit weapons, such as poverty, political instability, and the lack of effective governance. Ultimately, combatting the illegal arms trade is essential for promoting peace, security, and human rights on a global scale.

Efforts to Control the Global Arms Trade

The proliferation of weapons has significant implications for global security, human rights, and international stability. As conflicts and wars have prompted a surge in arms production and trade, the need for effective regulation has become increasingly pressing. Over the decades, various international agreements and initiatives have been established to control the global arms trade, aiming to mitigate its detrimental effects on societies and promote peace.

One of the most significant frameworks for controlling the arms trade is the Arms Trade Treaty (ATT), which was adopted by the United Nations General Assembly in April 2013 and entered into force in December 2014. The ATT regulates the international trade of conventional arms, including weapons, ammunition, and related equipment. Its primary objective is to prevent and eradicate the illicit trade and diversion of arms that can fuel armed conflict and facilitate human rights abuses. The treaty mandates that countries assess the potential risks associated with arms exports, including whether the weapons could be used to commit genocide, war crimes, or other serious violations of international humanitarian law. Furthermore, the ATT encourages states to strengthen their national control systems and maintain transparency in their arms trade practices.

In addition to the ATT, the United Nations Programme of Action on Small Arms and Light Weapons (PoA), adopted in 2001, plays a crucial role in addressing the proliferation of small arms and light weapons (SALW), which are often the weapons of choice in conflicts and violent crime. The PoA emphasizes the need for states to implement measures to prevent the illicit trade of SALW and to enhance cooperation in arms control efforts. It calls for improved stockpile management, effective marking and tracing of weapons, and international cooperation in combating the illicit arms trade.

Moreover, several regional agreements have been established to control arms trade within specific areas. For example, the Inter-American Convention Against the Illicit Manufacturing of and Trafficking in Firearms, Ammunition, Explosives and Other Related Materials, known as the CIFTA, aims to combat the illicit manufacture and trafficking of firearms in the Americas. Similarly, the African Union's Silencing the Guns initiative seeks to address the root causes of conflicts and reduce the proliferation of arms across the continent.

Despite these efforts, challenges remain in the effective implementation and enforcement of arms control agreements. One significant obstacle is the presence of the illicit arms trade, which operates outside the boundaries of legal frameworks and undermines efforts to regulate the global arms market. Illicit trade can thrive in regions afflicted by weak governance, corruption, and ongoing conflict, making it difficult to monitor and control the flow of weapons. Furthermore, the involvement of non-state actors and terrorist organizations in the arms trade complicates international efforts to establish comprehensive regulations.

To address these challenges, the global community must enhance cooperation and coordination among states, civil society, and international organizations. Building capacity in developing countries to implement arms control measures is also essential, as many lack the resources and infrastructure to effectively monitor and regulate arms trade. Additionally, fostering public awareness and advocacy for arms control issues can play a crucial role in promoting accountability and transparency in the arms trade.

In conclusion, while significant strides have been made through international agreements like the ATT and the PoA, the fight against the global arms trade remains a complex and ongoing challenge. Continued efforts to strengthen international cooperation, enhance regulatory frameworks, and combat illicit trade are vital in moving toward a more secure and peaceful world, free from the devastating impacts of uncontrolled arms proliferation.

Chapter 17

Weapons and Human Rights

The Human Cost of Weapons

Throughout history, the development and use of weapons have had profound implications for civilian populations caught in the crossfire of conflict. The impact of warfare on non-combatants is a critical aspect of the human cost of weapons, revealing the devastating consequences that arise when military technology escalates and conflicts erupt. While battles rage between armed forces, the realities faced by civilians—who often bear the brunt of warfare—are marked by suffering, displacement, and loss.

The use of weapons in warfare has evolved significantly over time, with each advancement bringing new threats to civilian safety. For instance, the introduction of artillery and aerial bombardment in World War I marked a turning point, as these weapons could reach beyond the front lines, resulting in widespread destruction in populated areas. Cities became battlegrounds, and civilians were subjected to indiscriminate attacks, leading to significant casualties and injuries. The infamous bombing campaigns of World War II, such as those on Dresden and Hiroshima, showcased the immense lethality of modern weaponry, where civilian areas were obliterated in the name of military strategy. These incidents underscore a grim reality: as military capabilities expand, so too does the potential for civilian harm.

Moreover, the proliferation of weapons, particularly small arms, has contributed to ongoing violence in post-conflict societies. In many regions, the availability of firearms has fueled cycles of violence, leading to crimes and conflicts that disproportionately affect civilians. For instance, in war-torn countries such as Syria and Yemen, the ease of access to weapons has exacerbated humanitarian crises, resulting in staggering numbers of civilian casualties. The collapse of law and order in these regions often leaves civilians vulnerable to armed groups and militias, who exploit the chaos for their gain.

The psychological impact of weaponry on civilians is another critical aspect of the human cost of warfare. Survivors of conflicts often endure long-lasting trauma resulting from the violence and instability that accompany armed confrontations. Children, in particular, are profoundly affected, facing disruptions to their education and development, and carrying the burden of witnessing atrocities. The psychological scars left by war can persist for generations, hindering recovery and reconciliation efforts within communities.

The use of weapons in conflicts has also led to significant displacement, with millions of civilians forced to flee their homes to escape violence. Refugee crises, such as those stemming from the Syrian Civil War, illustrate the far-reaching consequences of warfare on civilian populations. Displaced individuals often face dire conditions in refugee camps, lacking access to basic necessities such as food, clean water, and medical care. The strain on host countries and communities can lead to further tensions and violence, highlighting the interconnected nature of weapon use and its impact on societal stability.

Furthermore, the proliferation of weapons of mass destruction (WMD), including nuclear, biological, and chemical weapons, poses an existential threat to civilian populations. The use of such weapons in conflicts can lead to catastrophic humanitarian crises, with the potential for mass casualties and long-term environmental damage. The fear of WMD has prompted international efforts to regulate and control their proliferation, yet the threat remains significant, particularly in volatile regions.

In conclusion, the human cost of weapons extends far beyond the battlefield. Civilians are often the unintended victims of military conflict, facing immediate threats to their safety and long-term consequences for their health, well-being, and social stability. As the nature of warfare continues to evolve, it is imperative that the international community prioritizes the protection of civilians and seeks to mitigate the impact of weapons on non-combatants. Understanding the human cost of warfare is crucial in shaping policies that not only address the realities of conflict but also promote peace and security for all.

The Use of Weapons in Genocide and Ethnic Cleansing

The history of genocide and ethnic cleansing is marked by tragic episodes of systematic violence against specific groups, where the use of weapons has been a critical factor in the perpetration of such atrocities. This section delves into how weapons—ranging from small arms to heavier military hardware—have been employed to facilitate mass killings, oppression, and the erasure of cultural identities.

Historical Context

Genocides and ethnic cleansings are not solely modern phenomena; they have existed throughout history. However, the 20th century witnessed some of the most egregious instances, particularly with the advent of more sophisticated weaponry. Events such as the

Holocaust, the Rwandan Genocide, and the ethnic cleansing in the former Yugoslavia highlight how weapons have been integral to the execution of genocidal policies.

Mechanisms of Violence

The use of firearms, artillery, and in some cases, chemical weapons, has been central to the effectiveness of genocidal campaigns. In the Rwandan Genocide of 1994, for instance, the Hutu militia used machetes and small arms to carry out mass killings against the Tutsi population. The availability of rifles facilitated these acts of violence, allowing perpetrators to inflict harm rapidly and at a distance. Moreover, the use of weapons in such contexts often serves to incite fear and terror among the targeted population, further entrenching the divide between groups.

In the Bosnian War (1992-1995), the systematic use of heavy artillery and sniper fire against civilian populations in besieged cities exemplified another dimension of weaponry in ethnic cleansing. The siege of Sarajevo resulted in thousands of deaths and injuries, with heavy weaponry being used indiscriminately against non-combatants. Such tactics not only led to immediate casualties but also aimed to demoralize and displace entire communities.

Psychological Impact

The psychological impact of weaponized violence in genocides cannot be understated. The sound of gunfire, the presence of armed troops, and the fear of imminent death contribute to a climate of terror that often leads to mass displacement. In many instances, the threat of violence prompts individuals to flee, creating refugees and internally displaced persons. The use of weapons thus extends beyond physical harm, affecting the social fabric and collective memory of communities.

Strategic Use of Weapons

Governments and armed groups often employ weapons strategically to achieve specific objectives related to ethnic cleansing. The arming of particular factions can facilitate a systematic approach to violence, wherein weapons are used to identify, isolate, and eliminate targeted groups. This is evident in the case of the Khmer Rouge in Cambodia, where the regime utilized firearms and other military equipment to systematically target perceived enemies, leading to the deaths of approximately 1.7 million people from 1975 to 1979.

International Response and Accountability

The role of international arms trade in the facilitation of genocide and ethnic cleansing raises critical ethical questions. The supply of weapons to regimes accused of committing genocide has often been a contentious issue, highlighting the complicity of external actors. Efforts to regulate arms sales and enforce embargoes during conflicts are essential in preventing the escalation of violence against vulnerable populations.

Conclusion

The use of weapons in genocide and ethnic cleansing is a stark reminder of the destructive potential of military technology when wielded without accountability or moral consideration. Understanding the role of weapons in these contexts is crucial for developing effective prevention strategies, promoting disarmament, and ensuring that those responsible for such atrocities are held accountable. The historical record underscores the need for vigilance and action to prevent the recurrence of such heinous acts, ensuring that weapons are not used as instruments of oppression but rather as tools for peace and security.

The Debate Over Landmines and Cluster Munitions

Landmines and cluster munitions have become emblematic of the broader ethical and humanitarian challenges posed by indiscriminate weapons. These types of munitions are characterized by their capacity to inflict harm on civilians long after hostilities have ceased, raising pressing concerns about their legality, morality, and the lasting impact on affected communities.

Landmines are explosive devices planted in the ground, designed to detonate when triggered by pressure, tripwires, or remote detonation. Their primary purpose is to impede enemy movement, protect strategic locations, or deter advancing forces. However, their indiscriminate nature means that they do not distinguish between combatants and civilians. Once laid, landmines can remain active for decades, creating a lethal hazard for unsuspecting individuals who may inadvertently trigger them. This has led to tragic consequences, especially in post-conflict societies, where returning civilians can become victims of these hidden threats.

The Ottawa Treaty, also known as the Mine Ban Treaty (1997), was a landmark international agreement that sought to eliminate landmines globally. It was born from growing awareness of the humanitarian crises caused by landmines, which have been responsible for thousands of civilian casualties each year. Signatories of the treaty committed to banning the use, production, and transfer of anti-personnel mines, as well as to the destruction of existing stockpiles. However, notable holdouts, including the United States, Russia, and China, have continued to stockpile and utilize landmines, undermining the treaty's objectives and perpetuating their use in modern conflicts.

Cluster munitions are another contentious area within the realm of indiscriminate weapons. These weapons release multiple smaller submunitions over a wide area, intended to target enemy forces or equipment. However, just like landmines, cluster munitions often fail to explode upon impact, leaving behind unexploded ordnance that poses a significant threat to civilians long after a conflict has ended. Reports from war-torn regions reveal that children, drawn to the colorful and seemingly benign shapes of unexploded submunitions, are particularly vulnerable.

In response to the humanitarian crisis tied to cluster munitions, the Convention on Cluster Munitions (CCM) was adopted in 2008. This treaty prohibits the use, production, transfer, and stockpiling of cluster munitions, aiming to eliminate their use and mitigate the dangers they pose to civilian populations. Despite this, many countries, including the United States and Russia, have not ratified the treaty, continuing to stockpile these weapons and use them in conflicts, further complicating global efforts to address the humanitarian fallout.

The debates surrounding landmines and cluster munitions often pivot on the balance between military necessity and humanitarian considerations. Proponents of their use argue that such weapons are legitimate tools for achieving military objectives, effectively deterring enemy movement and protecting forces. However, critics counter that the indiscriminate nature of these weapons, coupled with their long-term impact on civilian populations, renders their use unethical and unacceptable in modern warfare. The overwhelming consensus among humanitarian organizations and many nations is that the potential for civilian casualties and the long-lasting consequences of these munitions far outweigh any military advantages they may offer.

As the international community grapples with the implications of landmines and cluster munitions, the ongoing controversies highlight the need for continued advocacy for disarmament and the prioritization of humanitarian principles in military strategy. The challenge remains to balance national security interests with the responsibility to protect civilian lives and promote global peace.

Arms Control and Disarmament Efforts

Arms control and disarmament have been critical components of international relations and peacekeeping efforts since the aftermath of World War I. The devastation wrought by global conflicts has propelled nations to seek frameworks that manage and mitigate the risks associated with weapon proliferation. This section explores the historical evolution of arms control and disarmament efforts, assesses their effectiveness, and highlights challenges that persist in the contemporary landscape.

The origins of formal arms control can be traced back to the Treaty of Versailles in 1919, which aimed to limit the military capacities of Germany post-World War I. This treaty set a precedent for future disarmament agreements, although its effectiveness was undermined by the lack of enforcement mechanisms and the eventual rise of militarism in Europe. The interwar period saw various attempts at disarmament, including the Washington Naval Treaty (1922) and the Kellogg-Briand Pact (1928), which sought to limit naval armaments and outlaw war, respectively. However, these agreements often faltered due to non-compliance and the geopolitical realities of the time.

The onset of World War II underscored the limitations of pre-war disarmament efforts. In response, the post-war international community, particularly through the newly formed United Nations (UN), embraced arms control as a central tenet of global security. The UN's establishment of the Disarmament Commission in 1952 marked a commitment to negotiating treaties aimed at reducing armaments and promoting peace.

One of the landmark achievements in arms control came with the Nuclear Non-Proliferation Treaty (NPT) of 1968. The NPT created a framework for preventing the spread of nuclear weapons while promoting peaceful uses of nuclear energy. It established a distinction between nuclear-armed states and non-nuclear states, attempting to curb the arms race during the Cold War. The treaty has been reviewed at various intervals, with the 2015 Review Conference underscoring ongoing concerns about compliance and the need for nuclear disarmament.

The Cold War era saw several significant arms control agreements, including the Strategic Arms Limitation Talks (SALT I and II) and the Intermediate-Range Nuclear Forces Treaty (INF) of 1987. These treaties reflected a growing recognition among superpowers of the catastrophic potential of nuclear conflict. SALT I capped the number of nuclear weapons, while the INF eliminated an entire class of nuclear missiles from Europe. These agreements were pivotal in reducing tensions and curtailing the arms race, illustrating how dialogue and diplomacy can yield tangible results.

Despite these successes, arms control efforts have faced significant challenges. Geopolitical tensions, the emergence of non-state actors, and the proliferation of advanced technologies have complicated the landscape. The rise of new nuclear states and the potential for regional conflicts to escalate have raised alarms about the relevance of existing treaties. The collapse of the INF Treaty in 2019, primarily due to allegations of treaty violations, has intensified concerns about the future of arms control.

Moreover, the proliferation of small arms and light weapons presents a pervasive challenge. These weapons, often fueling conflicts in developing nations, are less regulated than larger conventional arms. Efforts like the UN Programme of Action on Small Arms and the Arms Trade Treaty (ATT) aim to address these issues, yet implementation remains inconsistent.

In conclusion, while arms control and disarmament efforts have made significant strides since the early 20th century, the complexities of modern warfare and international relations necessitate renewed commitment and innovative approaches. The effectiveness of these efforts hinges on robust verification mechanisms, international cooperation, and the willingness of states to prioritize global security over national interests. The path forward requires a collective acknowledgment of the dire consequences of unchecked armament and a commitment to dialogue, transparency, and accountability in reducing the global arsenal.

The Future of Weapons and Human Rights

As humanity advances technologically, the development of new weaponry continues to raise complex questions regarding human rights and ethical considerations. The intersection of military innovation, security needs, and human rights protection poses significant challenges for policymakers, military leaders, and civil society. This section delves into the ongoing struggle to balance these often conflicting priorities, particularly in an era marked by rapid advancements in military technology.

The Dilemma of Security vs. Human Rights

The primary challenge in addressing the future of weapons and human rights lies in finding a balance between the need for security and the protection of individual freedoms. Governments and militaries argue that the development of sophisticated weaponry—ranging from autonomous drones to advanced surveillance systems—is essential for national defense and counterterrorism efforts. However, the deployment of such technologies often leads to violations of civil liberties, including privacy rights and the potential for extrajudicial killings.

For instance, the use of drones in combat and surveillance has raised significant ethical concerns. While drones can minimize risks to military personnel by allowing remote engagement with targets, they also present risks of collateral damage and civilian casualties. Reports of drone strikes resulting in the deaths of innocent civilians have sparked outrage and highlighted the need for accountability and oversight mechanisms. As such technologies become more prevalent, the challenge of ensuring that they are employed in accordance with human rights standards becomes increasingly pressing.

Emerging Technologies and Human Rights Implications

The emergence of autonomous weapons systems (AWS) poses another serious challenge for human rights. These systems, capable of making life-and-death decisions without human intervention, raise profound ethical questions. The potential for AWS to operate in combat environments without meaningful human oversight could lead to violations of international humanitarian law, including the principles of distinction and proportionality, which are designed to protect civilians in armed conflict.

Moreover, the development of cyber weapons introduces new dimensions of risk. Cyberattacks can target critical infrastructure, disrupt essential services, and create chaos in civilian life, leading to significant human rights implications. The anonymity associated with cyber warfare complicates the accountability landscape, making it difficult to attribute responsibility for attacks and to hold perpetrators accountable.

The Role of International Law
International law plays a crucial role in framing the debate around weapons and human rights. Existing treaties, such as the Geneva Conventions and various arms control agreements, provide a foundation for protecting human rights in the context of armed conflict. However, the rapid pace of technological advancement often outstrips the ability of international legal frameworks to adapt and respond effectively.

Calls for new treaties or amendments to existing agreements that specifically address emerging weapon technologies are gaining momentum. Advocates argue that such measures are essential to ensure that human rights considerations are integrated into the development and deployment of new weapons. The Campaign to Stop Killer Robots, for instance, seeks a preemptive ban on fully autonomous weapons, emphasizing the need for human accountability in lethal decision-making.

The Path Forward
The future of weapons and human rights requires a multifaceted approach that prioritizes ethical considerations alongside security imperatives. Governments, civil society, and international organizations must collaborate to establish robust regulatory frameworks that promote accountability, transparency, and adherence to human rights norms.

Education and awareness-raising about the implications of new military technologies are also vital. Engaging diverse stakeholders, including technologists, ethicists, and human rights advocates, in discussions about the future of weaponry can help shape policies that reflect a commitment to protecting human dignity.

In conclusion, the ongoing struggle to balance security needs with human rights concerns will define the future landscape of weaponry. As technological advancements continue to evolve, so too must our approaches to governance, ensuring that the pursuit of security does not come at the cost of the fundamental rights and freedoms of individuals worldwide.

Chapter 18

The Role of Weapons in Peacekeeping and Security

Weapons in Peacekeeping Operations

The deployment of weapons in peacekeeping operations is a complex and often contentious issue. Peacekeeping missions, typically sanctioned by international bodies such as the United Nations, aim to maintain or restore peace in conflict-affected regions. While the primary goal is stability and security, the presence and use of weapons during these operations can evoke debates regarding their effectiveness and implications for peace versus violence.

At the core of peacekeeping missions is the principle of neutrality. Peacekeepers are tasked with monitoring ceasefires, protecting civilians, and facilitating humanitarian assistance. However, the nature of the weapons they carry can influence both the perception and reality of their role. On one hand, weapons serve as a deterrent against potential aggressors, providing peacekeepers with the ability to respond to immediate threats. For instance, armed peacekeepers can protect vulnerable populations from violence, disarm local militias, and provide security for humanitarian convoys. In this context, the presence of weapons can be seen as a tool for stability, offering a protective shield to civilians caught in the crossfire of ongoing conflicts.

However, the use of weapons in peacekeeping operations is fraught with challenges. The armed presence of peacekeepers can inadvertently escalate tensions, particularly if local populations view them as an occupying force rather than neutral mediators. Incidents of excessive force have raised ethical concerns and questioned the legitimacy of peacekeeping missions. For example, when peacekeepers engage in armed confrontations, even if justified, it can undermine their impartiality and lead to resentment among local communities. This dynamic complicates the peacekeepers' mission and can hinder long-term reconciliation efforts.

Moreover, the types of weapons employed in peacekeeping operations can vary significantly. Traditional military weapons—such as rifles, machine guns, and armored vehicles—are often necessary for ensuring the safety of peacekeepers. However, the use of heavy artillery or air support can escalate conflicts rather than resolve them, leading to collateral damage and further civilian casualties. This raises critical questions about the proportionality and appropriateness of armed responses in peacekeeping contexts.

The role of non-lethal weapons has emerged as an alternative approach to managing conflicts without resorting to deadly force. Tools such as tear gas, rubber bullets, and sound cannons aim to control crowds and deter violence while minimizing fatalities. The integration of non-lethal options into peacekeeping operations reflects a growing awareness of the need to balance security with humanitarian considerations. Nevertheless, the deployment of such weapons still requires careful oversight to ensure they are used ethically and effectively.

International law and regulations also play a crucial role in shaping how weapons are used in peacekeeping missions. The United Nations and other international bodies establish guidelines governing the use of force, emphasizing the need for peacekeepers to act in accordance with human rights standards. However, the interpretation and enforcement of these regulations can be inconsistent, leading to disparities in how missions are conducted across different regions.

In conclusion, while weapons are an integral part of peacekeeping operations, their use is a double-edged sword. They can serve as essential tools for maintaining security and protecting vulnerable populations, but they also have the potential to exacerbate tensions and undermine the mission's credibility. The challenge lies in striking a balance between the necessity of armed protection and the imperative of maintaining peace and neutrality. Ultimately, the effectiveness of peacekeeping operations hinges not only on the weapons at their disposal but also on the commitment to uphold ethical standards and prioritize the well-being of local communities. As peacekeeping continues to evolve in response to modern conflicts, the discourse surrounding the role of weapons will remain a vital component of ensuring lasting peace and stability.

Disarmament and Demobilization

Disarmament and demobilization are critical processes that follow the cessation of armed conflict, aimed at fostering peace and stability in post-war societies. The successful collection of weapons and the reintegration of combatants into civilian life are essential steps in preventing the resurgence of violence and ensuring long-term security. This section delves into the strategies, challenges, and implications of post-conflict weapon collection and combatant reintegration.

The Importance of Disarmament and Demobilization

In the aftermath of conflict, the proliferation of weapons poses a significant threat to stability. Armed groups may retain access to firearms, explosives, and other military equipment, creating an environment ripe for renewed violence, crime, and civil unrest. Disarmament is thus crucial in reducing the number of weapons in circulation, while demobilization focuses on transitioning former combatants back into civilian society. Together, these processes contribute to rebuilding trust, fostering reconciliation, and promoting social cohesion.

Strategies for Effective Weapon Collection

1. Voluntary Surrender Programs: Many post-conflict nations implement voluntary disarmament initiatives, which encourage combatants to surrender their weapons in exchange for incentives, such as financial aid, vocational training, or community support. Successful examples include the Disarmament, Demobilization, and Reintegration (DDR) programs established in countries like Mozambique and Sierra Leone.

2. Mandatory Collection Initiatives: In some cases, governments may mandate weapon collection, utilizing legal frameworks to facilitate the process. This approach often involves the establishment of designated collection points, where individuals can turn in weapons without fear of prosecution. The effectiveness of such mandatory initiatives is often heightened by public awareness campaigns that emphasize the benefits of disarmament.

3. Community Involvement: Engaging local communities is vital for ensuring the success of disarmament efforts. Community leaders can play a crucial role in motivating individuals to turn in their weapons. Initiatives that involve the community, such as local peacebuilding activities or cultural events, help foster an environment conducive to disarmament.

Challenges in Weapon Collection
While the goals of disarmament and demobilization are noble, several challenges impede successful implementation:

- **Stigmatization and Fear:** Former combatants may fear social ostracism or legal repercussions for surrendering their weapons, particularly in contexts where allegiance to armed groups is deeply ingrained. Ensuring confidentiality and providing assurances of non-retribution are critical to overcoming these barriers.

- **Logistical and Security Issues:** In post-conflict settings, logistical difficulties such as transportation, infrastructure damage, and ongoing security threats can hinder the collection process. Effective coordination among government agencies, international organizations, and non-governmental organizations (NGOs) is essential for addressing these challenges.

- **Cultural Factors:** Cultural attitudes towards weapons can complicate disarmament efforts. In some societies, weapons are viewed as symbols of power and protection. Programs must be culturally sensitive and recognize the significance of weapons in local contexts to foster acceptance of disarmament.

Reintegration of Combatants

Successful disarmament is inextricably linked to the reintegration of former combatants into society. This process often includes educational programs, skills training, and psychosocial support to assist individuals in adapting to civilian life. Without effective reintegration, former combatants may struggle to find employment and reintegrate into their communities, increasing the risk of rejoining armed groups.

Conclusion

Disarmament and demobilization are integral to the peacebuilding process in post-conflict societies. Through the collection of weapons and the reintegration of combatants, nations can pave the way for lasting peace and stability. However, the complexities involved necessitate careful planning, community engagement, and a multi-faceted approach to address the diverse challenges encountered during these critical phases of recovery. As history has shown, the successful management of disarmament and demobilization can significantly influence the trajectory of post-conflict societies, fostering a sustainable and peaceful future.

The Role of Non-Lethal Weapons in Modern Security

In contemporary security operations, the use of non-lethal weapons (NLWs) has become increasingly prominent, offering law enforcement and military personnel alternatives to traditional firearms. These weapons are designed to incapacitate individuals or disperse crowds without causing permanent injury or death, thereby addressing the growing demand for methods that reduce the potential for lethal outcomes in conflict situations.

Development of Non-Lethal Weapons

The evolution of non-lethal weapons can be traced back to the latter half of the 20th century, particularly during the social upheavals of the 1960s and 1970s. Governments and law enforcement agencies sought methods to manage civil unrest effectively while minimizing casualties. This led to the development of various NLWs, including tear gas, rubber bullets, and bean bag rounds, which aimed to incapacitate rather than kill.

Advancements in technology have further expanded the arsenal of non-lethal options available to security forces. Modern innovations include electric shock devices, such as Tasers, which deliver a controlled electrical charge to incapacitate a target temporarily. Additionally, acoustic weapons that emit high-decibel sounds to disorient crowds and water cannons that can disperse protesters without causing lasting harm have also emerged as viable alternatives for crowd control.

Applications in Crowd Control

Non-lethal weapons have found substantial application in crowd control scenarios, particularly during protests, riots, or large public gatherings. Their use is often justified by the need to balance the enforcement of law and order with the protection of civil rights. For instance, during large-scale protests, police forces may deploy tear gas or rubber bullets to disperse unruly crowds while striving to avoid excessive use of force.

The strategic implementation of NLWs allows law enforcement to manage situations effectively while reducing the risk of escalation into deadly confrontations. However, the use of such weapons is not without its controversies. Critics argue that even non-lethal measures can result in unintended fatalities or serious injuries, especially when misused or deployed inappropriately. The efficacy of these weapons also raises ethical questions regarding their impact on civil liberties and the potential for abuse by authorities.

Training and Policy Considerations
The effectiveness of non-lethal weapons is heavily dependent on the training provided to security personnel. Proper understanding and application of these tools are crucial in ensuring that they serve their intended purpose without escalating violence. Training programs must emphasize de-escalation tactics and the importance of using NLWs judiciously.

Policies governing the use of non-lethal weapons must be carefully crafted to establish clear guidelines and accountability mechanisms. This includes protocols for when and how to deploy these weapons, as well as monitoring and evaluating their effectiveness in real-world situations. Transparency in the use of NLWs can help build public trust and mitigate concerns regarding their potential for misuse.

Future Implications
As urban environments continue to grow and the complexity of social dynamics increases, the demand for effective, humane crowd control methods will likely rise. Non-lethal weapons represent a critical component of modern security strategies, providing a means to maintain order without resorting to lethal force. Ongoing research and development in this field will be essential to create more effective non-lethal options that can adapt to various scenarios.

Moreover, as societies grapple with the implications of policing and public safety, the role of non-lethal weapons will continue to evolve. Engaging with communities to understand their perspectives on security measures and incorporating feedback into policy development will be paramount in ensuring that the use of NLWs aligns with societal values and human rights considerations. Ultimately, the challenge will be to strike a balance between maintaining public order and upholding the principles of justice and dignity for all individuals.

The Challenge of Small Arms Proliferation
Small arms proliferation remains one of the most pressing challenges in contemporary global security, significantly contributing to conflict, violence, and instability. Defined as firearms that

can be carried by a single person and include weapons such as handguns, rifles, shotguns, and submachine guns, small arms are often the weapons of choice for both state and non-state actors in conflicts. Their relative affordability, ease of use, and accessibility make them particularly attractive to various groups, including insurgents, organized crime networks, and terrorist organizations.

The Scope of Proliferation

The proliferation of small arms is a multifaceted issue with roots in various social, economic, and political contexts. According to estimates, there are over 1 billion small arms in circulation globally, with millions more produced each year. The United Nations (UN) has recognized that these weapons are a primary tool for violence and conflict, accounting for a significant proportion of deaths in armed violence. Small arms are not only used by military forces but are also increasingly utilized by civilian populations, leading to an increased risk of gun-related homicides, suicides, and accidents.

Fueling Conflict and Violence

Small arms significantly contribute to both the initiation and perpetuation of conflict. In many cases, the availability of these weapons can escalate tensions in fragile societies, leading to armed confrontations. For example, during civil wars, access to small arms allows insurgent groups to challenge governmental authority, leading to prolonged violence and instability. The 1994 Rwandan Genocide is a tragic illustration of how small arms can facilitate mass atrocities; the widespread availability of machetes and firearms enabled rapid and widespread violence against the Tutsi population.

Moreover, small arms are often used in urban violence and organized crime. In regions plagued by poverty and inequality, the ready availability of firearms exacerbates social tensions and contributes to high rates of homicide and gang violence. Cities with loose gun regulations often see a correlation between firearm availability and rates of violent crime, highlighting the role of small arms in undermining public safety and governance.

Challenges in Regulation

Regulating small arms presents significant challenges for governments and international bodies. The illicit trade in small arms operates through complex networks that exploit gaps in legislation and enforcement. Many countries lack comprehensive laws that govern the sale, transfer, and ownership of firearms, making it easier for weapons to flow into conflict zones and criminal enterprises. Efforts to establish international norms, such as the UN Arms Trade Treaty (ATT), aim to regulate the trade of conventional arms, including small arms. However, the effectiveness of these treaties often depends on the political will of states to adhere to and enforce their commitments.

Furthermore, the proliferation of small arms is fueled by the high demand for weapons in conflict zones, often driven by economic interests. Arms dealers, both legal and illegal, can profit immensely from supplying these weapons to parties engaged in conflict, further complicating disarmament efforts.

The Path Forward

To effectively address the challenge of small arms proliferation, comprehensive strategies must be developed that encompass legal, social, and educational dimensions. This includes strengthening national laws regarding arms ownership, enhancing international cooperation to combat illegal arms trafficking, and promoting community-based disarmament initiatives. Education and awareness campaigns can also play a vital role in changing societal attitudes towards gun ownership and violence.

In conclusion, the proliferation of small arms remains a significant challenge that continues to fuel conflict and violence worldwide. Addressing this issue requires a multifaceted approach that involves legal reforms, international cooperation, and community engagement to mitigate the impact of these weapons on global security and human safety.

The Future of Global Security

The intricate relationship between weapons and diplomacy is a cornerstone of international relations and security efforts in the contemporary world. As states grapple with the complexities of global security, the evolution of weaponry continues to play a pivotal role in shaping diplomatic strategies and international dynamics. The future of global security will be defined by the interplay of advanced technological developments, shifting power balances, and the overarching need for effective diplomacy to mitigate conflict.

One of the most significant trends influencing the future of global security is the rapid advancement of military technologies. Autonomous weapons systems, artificial intelligence, and cyber capabilities are revolutionizing how nations approach warfare and defense. These technologies not only enhance the lethality and efficiency of military operations but also complicate the dynamics of deterrence and conflict resolution. As states invest in cutting-edge weaponry, the potential for arms races escalates, particularly in regions with historical tensions. This creates a pressing need for diplomatic dialogue and arms control agreements to prevent escalation and miscalculation.

Moreover, the proliferation of advanced weapons technologies can shift the balance of power in international relations. Countries that can harness these technologies may gain strategic advantages over their adversaries, prompting those adversaries to respond with their own military enhancements. This cycle of action and reaction underscores the importance of diplomacy in managing competition and fostering stability. Effective diplomatic initiatives that promote transparency in military capabilities can help build trust and mitigate fears of aggression among nations.

Another critical aspect of the future of global security is the role of non-state actors, including terrorist organizations and insurgent groups, in the global arms landscape. The accessibility of conventional and unconventional weapons enables these groups to challenge state authority and disrupt regional stability. As such, diplomatic efforts to curb the illicit arms trade and regulate the flow of weapons to non-state actors become increasingly essential. International agreements, such as the Arms Trade Treaty (ATT), are vital in establishing norms and standards for arms transfers, yet their effectiveness relies on the commitment of states to enforce compliance and engage in cooperative security measures.

The implications of climate change and resource scarcity also factor into the future of global security, as competition over dwindling resources can lead to conflict. Weapons will inevitably play a role in these disputes, making it essential for nations to employ diplomacy that emphasizes cooperation and conflict resolution. Multilateral frameworks that focus on sustainable development and shared resource management can help mitigate tensions and promote peaceful coexistence.

In this evolving landscape, the role of international organizations and alliances cannot be overstated. Institutions like the United Nations (UN) and regional organizations provide platforms for dialogue and negotiation, facilitating the establishment of norms surrounding weapon use and disarmament. These organizations can also mediate disputes and foster trust-building measures among nations, reinforcing the importance of diplomacy in addressing security challenges.

Ultimately, the future of global security will hinge on the delicate balance between military preparedness and diplomatic engagement. As nations navigate the complexities of a rapidly changing security environment, the integration of diplomacy into defense strategies will be critical in managing conflicts, promoting stability, and addressing the multifaceted challenges posed by modern weaponry. The ongoing evolution of weapons will continue to shape international relations, but the commitment to diplomacy will determine whether these advancements lead to cooperation or conflict. As history has shown, the most effective security strategies will be those that prioritize dialogue, understanding, and collaborative efforts to ensure a more secure and peaceful world.

Chapter 19

Weapons in the Age of Terrorism

The Use of Weapons by Terrorist Organizations

Terrorist organizations have evolved significantly over the past few decades, adapting their tactics and strategies to exploit vulnerabilities in both state and non-state actors. One of the critical aspects of their operations is the acquisition and utilization of weapons, which plays a pivotal role in their ability to execute attacks, instill fear, and further their ideological goals. Understanding how these groups obtain and employ weapons provides insight into the broader dynamics of modern conflict and security.

Acquisition of Weapons

Terrorist organizations acquire weapons through various means, reflecting the diverse nature of their operations and the environments in which they operate. Some of the primary methods of weapon acquisition include:

1. Black Market Transactions: The illegal arms trade is a significant source of weapons for terrorist groups. The black market is often flooded with surplus military equipment, small arms, and explosives, making it relatively easy for organizations to procure weapons without attracting attention. This illicit trade is facilitated by corrupt officials, traffickers, and the global demand for arms, which can be exploited by these groups.

2. Theft and Diversion: Many terrorist organizations engage in theft or diversion of weapons from military stockpiles or law enforcement agencies. For instance, conflicts in unstable regions often lead to the looting of military bases, where weapons can be seized and repurposed for terrorist activities. Additionally, attacks on arms depots or ambushes on military convoys have been employed to gain access to more sophisticated weaponry.

3. Support from State Actors: Some terrorist organizations receive direct support from sympathetic state actors or rogue nations that provide funding, training, and weapons. This support can manifest in various forms, from the supply of small arms to more advanced weaponry, such as anti-tank missiles or even surface-to-air missiles. Such state-sponsored programs can significantly enhance a terrorist group's operational capabilities.

4. Homegrown Manufacturing: In some cases, terrorist groups have developed the capacity to manufacture their own weapons. This can include improvised explosive devices (IEDs), which are often made from readily available materials, or more sophisticated weaponry that requires technical expertise. The proliferation of knowledge through the internet has made it easier for these organizations to design and produce weapons, thereby reducing their dependency on external sources.

Utilization of Weapons

Once acquired, the deployment of weapons by terrorist organizations is typically characterized by a focus on maximizing impact, both in terms of casualties and psychological effects. The following are some common methods of weapon utilization:

1. High-Profile Attacks: Terrorists often utilize weapons in high-profile attacks designed to garner attention and instill fear. These attacks can involve automatic firearms, explosive devices, or even vehicle ramming attacks. The objective is to create chaos, draw media coverage, and communicate a political message.

2. Asymmetric Warfare: Terrorist organizations use weapons in asymmetric warfare, where they exploit the element of surprise and target vulnerabilities in conventional military forces. This can involve ambushes, hit-and-run tactics, and the use of IEDs to inflict casualties on larger military or civilian targets.

3. Indiscriminate Violence: Many terrorist groups employ weapons indiscriminately to maximize civilian casualties. This strategy not only amplifies the psychological impact but also serves to polarize communities and provoke government reactions that may further their agenda.

4. Symbolic Use of Weapons: The choice of weaponry can also hold symbolic meaning. For example, the use of firearms instead of conventional military arms may signal a rejection of state authority and an embrace of guerrilla tactics.

In conclusion, the acquisition and use of weapons by terrorist organizations illustrate their adaptability and the complexities of modern conflict. Understanding these dynamics is essential for developing effective counter-terrorism strategies that not only focus on military responses but also address the underlying causes of terrorism and the networks that support these groups. As global security continues to evolve, the challenge of mitigating the threat posed by armed terrorist organizations remains a critical concern for nations worldwide.

The Threat of Nuclear, Biological, and Chemical Weapons

The evolution of warfare has seen the introduction of increasingly sophisticated and destructive technologies, none more alarming than weapons of mass destruction (WMD)—specifically, nuclear, biological, and chemical weapons. These forms of armament pose unique threats, not just from their potential for mass casualties, but also due to their geopolitical implications, ethical concerns, and the challenges they create for international security.

Nuclear Weapons

Nuclear weapons, which utilize nuclear reactions to release vast amounts of energy, represent one of the most profound existential threats to humanity. Since the bombings of Hiroshima and Nagasaki in 1945, the world has been acutely aware of the devastating power these weapons can unleash. The Cold War era was marked by a significant arms race, primarily between the United States and the Soviet Union, leading to the stockpiling of thousands of nuclear warheads. This arms race fostered a doctrine of mutually assured destruction (MAD), a precarious balance where both sides possessed the capability to inflict catastrophic damage on one another, thereby deterring direct conflict.

However, the threat posed by nuclear weapons extends beyond the superpowers. Today, several nations have acquired nuclear capabilities, and the potential for proliferation remains a critical concern. Rogue states and non-state actors pose an additional risk, as the desire for nuclear weapons can lead to regional instability and escalation of conflicts. The possibility of nuclear terrorism, where an extremist group might obtain a nuclear device or fissile material, adds an alarming dimension to contemporary security concerns.

Biological Weapons

Biological weapons utilize pathogens or toxins to cause disease and death in humans, animals, or plants. The historical use of biological agents, such as during World War I and in various conflicts throughout the 20th century, has highlighted their potential for mass casualties. However, advancements in biotechnology have raised the stakes significantly; synthetic biology now permits the engineering of pathogens with enhanced virulence or resistance to existing treatments.

The threat of bioterrorism, particularly following the anthrax attacks in the United States in 2001, has prompted governments to bolster their biodefense strategies. The global interconnectedness of today's world means that an outbreak could spread rapidly, leading to a public health crisis that transcends national borders. The ethical implications of developing biological weapons, particularly when considering advancements in genetic engineering, further complicate this issue.

Chemical Weapons

Chemical weapons, which include nerve agents, blister agents, and choking agents, are designed to incapacitate or kill through chemical reactions. Although their use is prohibited under the Chemical Weapons Convention (CWC), instances of chemical warfare have persisted, most notably in the Syrian civil war, highlighting the challenges of enforcement and compliance. The psychological impact of chemical weapons is profound, as they instill fear in civilian populations and are often perceived as weapons of terror.

The global community faces significant challenges in controlling and regulating the proliferation of chemical weapons. Despite international treaties, the clandestine nature of their development and stockpiling makes verification difficult. The use of chemical weapons in conflicts also raises questions about the efficacy of existing international laws and the mechanisms for accountability.

Conclusion

The ongoing threat posed by nuclear, biological, and chemical weapons necessitates a robust international response. The complexities of modern geopolitics, technological advancements, and the evolving nature of warfare demand that nations work collaboratively to address these challenges. Efforts to strengthen treaties, enhance verification mechanisms, and promote disarmament are critical. Moreover, the global community must grapple with the ethical implications of WMD development and deployment, striving to establish a balance between security and the preservation of human rights. As we advance into a future where these weapons remain a persistent threat, the quest for effective governance, accountability, and peace becomes all the more vital.

The Role of Technology in Counter-Terrorism

As terrorism has evolved into a complex and pervasive global threat, technology has become an indispensable tool in counter-terrorism efforts. The integration of advanced technological solutions not only enhances the capabilities of law enforcement and military agencies but also provides innovative approaches for preventing and responding to terrorist activities. This section explores the various ways in which technology is utilized in the fight against terrorism, highlighting advancements in surveillance, data analysis, communication, and weaponry.

Surveillance and Intelligence Gathering

One of the most significant advancements in counter-terrorism is the use of surveillance technology. Drones equipped with high-resolution cameras and sensors allow for real-time monitoring of suspected terrorist activities, enabling agencies to gather intelligence without the need for ground personnel. These unmanned aerial vehicles (UAVs) can cover vast areas, providing critical data that may inform tactical decisions and operational planning.

Additionally, closed-circuit television (CCTV) systems have been enhanced with facial recognition software, allowing law enforcement to identify and track individuals who may pose a threat. Such systems have been implemented in urban areas and at public events, where the risk of terrorist attacks is heightened. The ability to analyze footage in real time and cross-reference with databases of known offenders provides a powerful tool for preemptive action.

Data Analysis and Artificial Intelligence
The vast amounts of data generated in today's digital age present both challenges and opportunities for counter-terrorism. Advanced data analytics, powered by artificial intelligence (AI) and machine learning, enable agencies to sift through massive datasets to identify patterns and anomalies that might indicate terrorist planning or activity. Predictive analytics can assess behavioral trends, allowing for early detection of potential threats.

Moreover, social media platforms are monitored for extremist content and recruitment efforts. Algorithms can analyze posts and interactions to identify individuals who may be radicalized or connected to terrorist groups. This proactive approach aids in disrupting potential attacks before they can be carried out.

Communication Technologies
Secure communication technologies play a crucial role in both terrorist operations and counter-terrorism efforts. While terrorist organizations increasingly use encrypted messaging apps to coordinate activities and evade detection, counter-terrorism agencies are developing their own secure channels to share intelligence and operational plans. The challenge lies in balancing the need for security with the protection of civil liberties, as the use of intrusive surveillance can lead to public backlash and potential abuse.

Additionally, technology-enhanced collaboration between international agencies has become vital in combating transnational terrorism. Platforms that facilitate information sharing and joint operations allow countries to collaborate more effectively, pooling resources and expertise to address the global nature of the threat.

Advanced Weaponry and Tactical Innovations
Technological advancements have also transformed the tools and tactics used in counter-terrorism operations. Smart weapons, equipped with precision-guidance systems, allow

for targeted strikes that minimize collateral damage while effectively neutralizing threats. For example, the use of drones in military operations has enabled targeted assassinations of high-profile terrorist leaders, significantly disrupting their organizational capabilities.

Furthermore, non-lethal weapons, such as tasers and riot control technologies, are increasingly employed in situations where lethal force is not warranted. This reflects a growing recognition of the need for a nuanced approach to counter-terrorism, where the objective is not only to eliminate threats but also to maintain public safety and trust.

Conclusion

In conclusion, technology plays a transformative role in counter-terrorism, providing agencies with the tools needed to adapt to the evolving threat landscape. Surveillance systems, data analytics, secure communications, and advanced weaponry collectively enhance the capability to prevent and respond to terrorist activities. However, as technology continues to advance, it also presents new challenges, particularly concerning privacy, civil liberties, and ethical considerations. Striking a balance between effective counter-terrorism measures and the protection of individual rights remains a critical task for policymakers and society as a whole.

Cyberterrorism

In the 21st century, the landscape of warfare and terrorism has been profoundly reshaped by the advent of digital technology. Cyberterrorism, defined as the politically motivated use of the internet to conduct violent acts against individuals or groups, has emerged as a significant threat, leveraging the interconnectedness of our digital world to cause chaos and fear. This chapter explores how cyberattacks have evolved into a tool for terror, the methods employed, and the implications for global security.

Cyberterrorism operates on the premise that information systems can be targeted to achieve political or ideological objectives. Unlike traditional terrorism, which often relies on physical violence, cyberterrorism exploits vulnerabilities in computer networks and systems to disrupt infrastructure, steal sensitive information, and instill fear among populations. High-profile attacks, such as the 2007 cyber assaults on Estonia and the 2010 Stuxnet worm that targeted Iran's nuclear facilities, exemplify the potential for cyberattacks to achieve strategic objectives that were once the domain of kinetic warfare.

The motivations behind cyberterrorism are varied, but they often stem from extremist ideologies or political grievances. Terrorist organizations, such as ISIS and al-Qaeda, have increasingly embraced digital platforms to recruit, radicalize, and coordinate operations. They utilize social media to disseminate propaganda, but they also engage in cyberattacks to further their agendas. For instance, ISIS has claimed responsibility for a series of cyberattacks against various institutions, including government websites and private sector infrastructure, using the internet to amplify the impact of their message and intimidate adversaries.

The methods of cyberterrorism are diverse, ranging from Distributed Denial of Service (DDoS) attacks, where multiple systems are used to flood a target's network and render it inoperable, to ransomware attacks that encrypt data and demand payment for its release. Additionally, data breaches can lead to the exposure of sensitive information, threatening national security and compromising personal data. The anonymity of the internet makes it challenging to attribute these attacks accurately, complicating the response from authorities and law enforcement agencies.

One of the most alarming aspects of cyberterrorism is its potential to target critical infrastructure, such as power grids, transportation systems, and healthcare facilities. An attack on these essential services could have catastrophic consequences, leading to widespread disruption, economic damage, and loss of life. The 2020 cyberattack on the U.S. health sector during the COVID-19 pandemic highlights the vulnerability of healthcare systems, underscoring the pressing need for robust cybersecurity measures.

Governments and organizations worldwide are increasingly recognizing the necessity of cybersecurity as a critical component of national security. Strategies have been developed to enhance cyber defenses, promote public-private partnerships, and improve resilience against potential cyber threats. International cooperation is essential, as cyberterrorism often transcends national boundaries, requiring a unified approach to effectively combat this evolving threat.

However, the fight against cyberterrorism poses significant challenges. The rapid pace of technological innovation often outstrips the ability of regulatory frameworks and security measures to keep pace. Moreover, the dual-use nature of many technologies means that tools developed for legitimate purposes can also be exploited for malicious intent.

In conclusion, cyberterrorism represents a new frontier in the landscape of modern warfare and terrorism, with profound implications for global security. As the digital realm continues to expand, so too will the potential for cyberattacks to serve as instruments of terror. Addressing this challenge requires a multifaceted approach that combines advanced technological solutions, international cooperation, and a commitment to preserving the principles of security and human rights in an increasingly interconnected world. The evolution of cyberterrorism as a weapon underscores the necessity for vigilance and preparedness in the face of emerging threats.

The Global Response to Terrorism

Modern terrorism poses complex challenges that require nations to adapt their military and security strategies in response to evolving threats. The global landscape of terrorism has shifted dramatically in the 21st century, characterized by a rise in asymmetric warfare, decentralized operational structures, and the utilization of advanced technology by terrorist organizations. In response, states have developed a multifaceted approach that encompasses military, intelligence, diplomatic, and legal measures to combat these threats effectively.

One of the most prominent adaptations has been the evolution of military tactics. Traditional warfare, characterized by large-scale engagements between states and organized armies, has been supplanted by the need for specialized counterterrorism operations. Nations have focused on developing elite special operations forces capable of rapid deployment and precision strikes against high-value targets, including terrorist leaders and infrastructure. The United States, for example, has significantly invested in units like SEAL Team Six and Delta Force, which are trained to conduct covert operations in hostile environments.

Furthermore, counterterrorism tactics have increasingly integrated intelligence-gathering capabilities with military action. The modern battlefield is as much about information as it is about firepower. Nations now prioritize intelligence, surveillance, and reconnaissance (ISR) capabilities to identify and track terrorist networks before they can execute an attack. Technologies such as drones equipped with advanced sensors and cameras enable real-time monitoring and intelligence collection. The use of unmanned aerial vehicles (UAVs) for targeted strikes has become a hallmark of contemporary counterterrorism efforts, allowing military forces to engage targets with minimal risk to personnel and collateral damage.

In addition, nations have adapted their legal frameworks and policies to address the nuances of terrorism. The challenge of balancing civil liberties with national security has led to the establishment of new laws that empower law enforcement agencies to surveil and detain suspects more effectively. Anti-terrorism legislation, such as the USA PATRIOT Act in the United States, has expanded the government's ability to intercept communications and conduct investigations. Similar legislative measures have been adopted globally, reflecting a consensus on the need to enhance legal tools against terrorism while sparking debates about civil rights and privacy.

Another critical response has been the emphasis on international cooperation and intelligence-sharing. Terrorism is a transnational challenge that often transcends borders, requiring nations to work collaboratively to disrupt networks and prevent attacks. Organizations such as INTERPOL and initiatives like the Global Counterterrorism Forum facilitate the exchange of information and best practices among nations. Joint military operations, such as those conducted against ISIS in Iraq and Syria, demonstrate the importance of multinational coalitions in addressing shared threats.

Moreover, the role of technology in counter-terrorism has expanded beyond military applications. Cybersecurity has become a critical frontier in the fight against terrorism, as terrorist groups increasingly exploit the internet for recruitment, propaganda, and operational planning. Nations have ramped up efforts to combat cyberterrorism by strengthening their cyber defenses and developing offensive cyber capabilities to disrupt terrorist communications and activities online.

Finally, the global response to terrorism also involves addressing the root causes of extremism through diplomatic and developmental strategies. Countries recognize that military action alone cannot eliminate the underlying grievances that fuel terrorism. Efforts to promote education, economic opportunities, and political inclusion in vulnerable communities are essential components of a comprehensive approach to counter radicalization.

In summary, the global response to terrorism has evolved into a complex interplay of military tactics, legal frameworks, intelligence-sharing, technological advancements, and proactive measures to address root causes. As the nature of terrorism continues to evolve, nations must remain adaptable and responsive to emerging threats while upholding the principles of justice and human rights. The balance between security and civil liberties will remain a central challenge in the ongoing struggle against terrorism in the modern world.

Chapter 20

Conclusion

The Continuous Evolution of Weaponry

The history of weaponry is a reflection of humanity's quest for survival, power, and dominance. From the rudimentary stone tools of early humans to the sophisticated artificial intelligence (AI) systems of today, the evolution of weapons has been a complex interplay of technological innovation, cultural shifts, and social demands. Each significant advancement in weaponry has not only transformed military tactics but has also influenced societal structures, economies, and international relations.

Initially, weaponry was closely tied to survival and hunting. The first tools, made from stone, were adapted for defense and hunting, marking the transition from mere survival to the establishment of social hierarchies based on access to these tools. As societies evolved, so did their weapons. The development of spears, clubs, and subsequently the bow and arrow represented crucial turning points, enabling humans to engage in combat from a distance and altering the dynamics of warfare.

With the advent of metallurgy, the Bronze Age heralded a new era in weapon-making. Bronze not only provided strength and durability but also allowed for the creation of more complex weapons, such as swords and chariots, which revolutionized battlefield strategies. The transition to iron during the Iron Age further enhanced weapon efficiency, leading to the rise of powerful empires that leveraged superior weaponry for conquest.

The Classical and Medieval periods saw the refinement of weapons and tactics. The phalanx formation and Roman legions exemplified organized warfare, while advancements like the longbow and crossbow introduced new principles of ranged combat. The emergence of gunpowder in the late Middle Ages marked another monumental shift, as it rendered traditional weaponry obsolete, paving the way for firearms and artillery that would dominate the battlefield for centuries.

The Industrial Revolution ushered in mass production and mechanization, fundamentally altering the scale and nature of warfare. The introduction of rifled firearms and machine guns in the late 19th and early 20th centuries escalated the lethality of conflicts, as seen in the devastating trench warfare of World War I. The interwar period further refined military technology, with innovations in tanks, aircraft, and naval power shaping strategies for World War II and beyond.

In the post-war era, the Cold War introduced the concept of Mutually Assured Destruction (MAD) and the development of nuclear weapons, which transformed global geopolitics. The intricate web of arms races and treaties underscored the dual nature of weaponry as both a tool for national defense and a potential harbinger of global catastrophe.

As we moved into the 21st century, new technologies began to emerge, reshaping the landscape of warfare once again. Precision-guided munitions, drones, and cyber warfare have introduced unprecedented levels of accuracy and stealth, allowing for targeted strikes with minimal collateral damage. The rise of autonomous weapons and directed-energy systems is poised to further redefine combat, raising ethical questions about the role of AI in decision-making processes during warfare.

Looking to the future, the continuous evolution of weaponry raises critical issues. The development of hypersonic weapons and the potential for space-based weapons are indicators of an ongoing arms race that may shift conflict dynamics once again. Moreover, the ethical implications of these technologies, such as accountability in autonomous systems and the risks associated with cyber warfare, will challenge policymakers and society at large.

In conclusion, the history of weaponry is not merely a chronicle of technological advancements but a reflection of humanity's broader narrative—its conflicts, aspirations, and moral dilemmas. As we navigate the complexities of modern warfare, it is imperative that we consider not only the advancements in weapon technology but also their profound impact on society, ethics, and global security. Balancing innovation with responsibility will be vital to ensuring that the evolution of weaponry serves as a tool for peace rather than a catalyst for destruction.

Ethical Considerations in Future Weapon Development

As technological advancements continue to reshape the landscape of warfare, ethical considerations surrounding the development of new weaponry have become increasingly paramount. Emerging technologies such as artificial intelligence (AI), autonomous weapons systems, hypersonic missiles, and directed-energy weapons challenge traditional ethical frameworks, raising complex questions about the morality of their use, the potential for unintended consequences, and the broader implications for humanity.

One of the most pressing ethical concerns is the rise of autonomous weapons, often referred to as "killer robots." These systems can operate independently of human intervention, making life-and-death decisions based on algorithms and programmed criteria. The moral implications of delegating such critical decisions to machines are profound. Critics argue that removing human judgment from the battlefield undermines accountability and diminishes the moral weight of military decisions. If an autonomous weapon erroneously targets civilians or misidentifies a threat, who bears responsibility? This lack of accountability poses significant challenges for international humanitarian law, which is rooted in the principles of distinction and proportionality.

Additionally, the potential for bias in AI systems raises ethical alarms. Machine learning algorithms are trained on historical data, which may contain biases reflecting societal prejudices. If these biases are not addressed, autonomous weapons could perpetuate discrimination, targeting marginalized groups or exacerbating existing conflicts. The ethical implications extend beyond the battlefield; they raise concerns about the misuse of technology in domestic law enforcement and surveillance, where similar biases could lead to systemic injustice.

The development of hypersonic weapons presents another ethical dilemma, primarily due to their speed and potential for devastating consequences. These weapons could drastically reduce warning times for adversaries, increasing the risk of miscalculations and accidental conflicts. The principle of proportionality in warfare—ensuring that military actions are proportionate to the threat—becomes increasingly difficult to apply when decisions must be made within seconds. The ethical implications of initiating conflict based on rapid-response technologies necessitate a re-examination of existing military doctrines and the legal frameworks governing warfare.

Directed-energy weapons, such as lasers, offer precision and reduced collateral damage, but they also raise ethical questions about their deployment. The potential for these weapons to be used in crowd control or against civilian populations presents a moral dilemma. The line between legitimate military target and civilian harm can become blurred, challenging the ethical justifications for their use. Furthermore, the accessibility of these technologies could lead to their proliferation among non-state actors, raising fears of misuse in terrorism or asymmetric warfare.

The ethical landscape of future weapon development is further complicated by the geopolitical implications of emerging technologies. Nations are in a race to achieve technological superiority, often prioritizing military advancements over ethical considerations. This arms race exacerbates global tensions and undermines international treaties aimed at weapon regulation and disarmament.

In conclusion, as we forge ahead into an era characterized by rapid technological advancement, it is imperative that ethical considerations guide the development and deployment of new weaponry. Policymakers, military leaders, technologists, and ethicists must engage in robust dialogues to establish frameworks that prioritize accountability, prevent bias, and ensure compliance with humanitarian principles. The challenges posed by autonomous systems, hypersonic weapons, and directed-energy technologies demand not only innovative solutions but also a commitment to uphold the moral obligations of warfare. By addressing these ethical considerations, we can strive to ensure that technological advancements serve humanity, rather than compromise our fundamental values.

The Role of International Law in Weapon Regulation

International law plays a crucial role in regulating the development, proliferation, and use of weapons, shaping the landscape of global security and humanitarian norms. The intricate framework of treaties, conventions, and customary law aims to balance state sovereignty, security interests, and humanitarian considerations in the context of armed conflict. As weapon technology evolves, so too does the necessity for a robust legal framework that can effectively address emerging threats and challenges.

One of the foundational pillars of international law regarding weapons is the Geneva Conventions, which establish rules for the humane treatment of individuals during armed conflict. These conventions, alongside their Additional Protocols, outline the protections afforded to non-combatants and the restrictions on the types of weapons that can be employed. For instance, the use of weapons that cause unnecessary suffering or have indiscriminate effects is explicitly prohibited. This principle is a significant aspect of international humanitarian law (IHL), which seeks to limit the effects of armed conflict by safeguarding those who are not participating in hostilities.

In addition to the Geneva Conventions, various treaties specifically address particular categories of weapons. The Chemical Weapons Convention (CWC), for example, prohibits the development, production, and stockpiling of chemical weapons, reflecting a global consensus on the horrors associated with their use. Similarly, the Biological Weapons Convention (BWC) aims to prevent the development and stockpiling of biological agents for warfare. The Ottawa Treaty, aimed at banning landmines, and the Convention on Cluster Munitions (CCM), which seeks to eliminate cluster munitions, are further examples of international legal efforts to address specific weaponry that poses significant humanitarian risks.

The Arms Trade Treaty (ATT), adopted in 2013, represents a landmark effort to regulate the international trade in conventional weapons. It aims to establish common standards for the transfer of arms, ensuring that they are not used to fuel conflict, violate human rights, or contribute to international instability. The ATT emphasizes the importance of assessing the potential impact of arms transfers on peace and security, advocating for responsible arms trading practices among states.

However, the effectiveness of international law in weapon regulation is often challenged by state sovereignty and political will. While treaties and conventions provide legal frameworks, their enforcement relies heavily on the willingness of states to comply and implement their provisions. Non-signatory states or those that evade compliance can undermine collective efforts to regulate weapons effectively. Moreover, the proliferation of non-state actors, including terrorist organizations and insurgent groups, complicates the enforcement of international legal standards, as these entities often operate outside the purview of state control.

Emerging technologies, such as autonomous weapons systems and cyber warfare capabilities, pose new challenges to existing international legal frameworks. The rapid development of these technologies outpaces the ability of international law to address their implications adequately. As a result, discussions are underway in various international forums, including the United Nations, to explore how existing treaties can be adapted or new frameworks developed to govern these advancements.

As we look to the future, the role of international law in weapon regulation will be increasingly vital in addressing the dual challenges of advancing technology and persistent global conflict. Continuous dialogue among nations, alongside robust mechanisms for transparency and accountability, will be essential in shaping a legal landscape that promotes peace, security, and respect for human rights in the face of evolving weaponry. Balancing the interests of national security with humanitarian principles will remain a complex but necessary task for the international community as it navigates the future of warfare and weapon regulation.

Preparing for the Unknown

As we stand on the precipice of the future, the evolution of weaponry continues to challenge our understanding of international security and ethical governance. The rapid advancement of technology has not only transformed the nature of warfare but has also introduced a myriad of emerging threats that we must prepare for. Speculating on these potential challenges is crucial for developing effective strategies to mitigate risks and safeguard global stability.

One of the most pressing threats on the horizon is the rise of autonomous weapons systems, commonly referred to as "killer robots." These AI-driven machines are capable of making decisions without human intervention, raising significant ethical and operational concerns. The potential for autonomous drones and ground vehicles to conduct warfare independently could lead to conflicts escalating uncontrollably, as machines may operate faster than human commanders can respond. The delegation of life-and-death decisions to algorithms poses moral dilemmas, where accountability for actions becomes murky. This necessitates the development of robust international legal frameworks to govern the use of such technologies and ensure compliance with humanitarian principles.

Another emerging challenge is the proliferation of cyber warfare capabilities. As nations increasingly rely on digital infrastructure, the potential for cyber attacks to disrupt critical services, steal sensitive information, or manipulate public perception grows exponentially. State-sponsored hacking, as witnessed in various geopolitical tensions, demonstrates how cyber tools can be weaponized to achieve strategic objectives without direct military engagement. As technology continues to advance, the sophistication and impact of cyber threats will likely escalate, necessitating a comprehensive approach that includes both defensive measures and international cooperation to deter state-sponsored cyber aggression.

The specter of biological warfare also looms larger in our interconnected world. Advances in biotechnology, while offering remarkable potential for medical breakthroughs, also raise concerns about their misuse. The ability to engineer pathogens or manipulate existing ones could lead to the development of novel biological weapons, potentially causing catastrophic consequences. The COVID-19 pandemic has underscored the vulnerabilities inherent in global public health systems and the dire need for robust surveillance and response mechanisms. To combat this emerging threat, international collaboration is key, with a focus on establishing strict biosecurity protocols and enhancing global health infrastructure to prevent the weaponization of biological agents.

In addition to these technological advancements, the potential for space-based weaponry presents an entirely new arena of conflict. As nations vie for dominance in space, the militarization of this domain could lead to the deployment of weapons capable of targeting satellites and other space assets. Such conflicts could disrupt global communications, navigation, and surveillance systems, with cascading effects on everyday life and economic stability. Establishing treaties to demilitarize space and promote cooperative exploration will be essential in mitigating the risks associated with this emerging frontier.

Lastly, the rise of non-state actors and extremist groups, particularly in conflict-ridden regions, presents an ongoing challenge. These groups often exploit modern weaponry and technology to further their agendas, utilizing asymmetric warfare tactics that complicate traditional military responses. The ability of these actors to acquire advanced weaponry through illicit channels necessitates a multifaceted approach that includes intelligence sharing, capacity building for local security forces, and addressing the underlying socio-political grievances that fuel extremism.

In conclusion, preparing for the unknown requires a proactive approach that anticipates and addresses the multifaceted threats posed by emerging technologies and geopolitical dynamics. International cooperation, robust legal frameworks, and ethical considerations must guide the development and deployment of new weapon systems. By fostering dialogue and collaboration among nations, we can navigate the complexities of modern warfare and work towards a more secure and stable world. The future of global security hinges on our ability to adapt, innovate, and respond to these evolving challenges.

Final Thoughts

As we reflect on the extensive history of weaponry—from primitive stone tools to sophisticated autonomous systems—it becomes increasingly clear that the evolution of weapons is intertwined with the fundamental aspects of human nature, society, and ethics. The development of weapons has always been driven by the dual imperatives of security and power; however, the implications of this relationship raise complex ethical considerations that must be addressed in our contemporary world.

Throughout history, weapons have served as instruments of protection, enabling societies to defend themselves against external threats. Yet, they have also been tools of oppression, contributing to violence and conflict. The balance between using weapons for legitimate defense and the potential for misuse or escalation into violence is a delicate one. As technology advances, this dichotomy becomes even more pronounced.

In the modern context, the advent of sophisticated weaponry—such as nuclear arms, chemical weapons, and autonomous drones—poses unprecedented ethical dilemmas. The destructive potential of these technologies raises serious questions about the morality of their development and use. For instance, the principle of proportionality in warfare, which mandates that the harm caused by military actions must be proportional to the military advantage gained, becomes increasingly challenging to apply with weapons that can cause mass destruction indiscriminately.

Moreover, the rise of cyber warfare and the potential for cyberterrorism introduce a new layer of complexity to the balance between security and humanity. Cyberattacks can target critical infrastructure, disrupt daily life, and cause panic without traditional combat. The anonymity and reach of cyber weapons blur the lines between combatants and civilians, raising ethical concerns about collateral damage and the protection of non-combatants.

As governments and military organizations strive to safeguard their nations, they must also grapple with the moral implications of their actions. The arms race during the Cold War is a poignant example; nations prioritized security through deterrence, often at the expense of global stability and ethical considerations. The doctrine of mutually assured destruction (MAD) exemplified how the pursuit of security could lead to a precarious and ethically troubling status quo.

In light of these challenges, international law and treaties play a pivotal role in shaping the discourse surrounding weapon development. Initiatives such as the Treaty on the Non-Proliferation of Nuclear Weapons (NPT) and the Arms Trade Treaty (ATT) seek to regulate the proliferation and use of weapons, promoting accountability and ethical standards. However, compliance and enforcement remain significant hurdles, often undermined by national interests and geopolitical tensions.

As we look to the future, the challenge lies in balancing the need for security with the imperative to uphold human rights and ethical standards. Advancements in weaponry must be accompanied by a robust ethical framework that considers the implications of their use. This involves fostering dialogue among nations, civil society, and ethicists to ensure that the development of new weapons technologies aligns with humanitarian principles.

Ultimately, the ongoing evolution of weaponry invites us to reflect on our values as a society. The balance between security and humanity is not merely a political or military concern; it is a moral imperative that shapes our collective identity. As we navigate the complexities of modern warfare, it is essential to prioritize ethical considerations, ensuring that the quest for security does not compromise our commitment to humanity. In doing so, we can strive for a future where weapons serve as tools of protection rather than instruments of destruction, fostering a world where peace and security coexist harmoniously with ethical integrity.

Printed in Great Britain
by Amazon